A Wild Life And
A Dog Called Brown

Rose and Brown in the Kluane Front Ranges, ca. 2018, on a trip out by helicopter to help the Surficial Geologists at Yukon Geological Survey.

A Wild Life And
A Dog Called Brown

A Memoir written by
Maggie Squires

CCB Publishing
British Columbia, Canada

A Wild Life And A Dog Called Brown

Copyright ©2024, 2025 by Maggie Squires
ISBN-13 978-1-77143-623-6
Second Edition

Library and Archives Canada Cataloguing in Publication
Title: A wild life and a dog called Brown / by Maggie Squires.
Names: Squires, Maggie, 1954- author.
Issued in print and electronic formats.
ISBN 9781771436236 (softcover) – ISBN 9781771436243 (PDF)
Additional cataloguing data available from Library and Archives Canada

Front cover illustration credit: "An old Brown rests on an ancient rock," acrylic on canvas © 2021. At rest in the mountains of his summer romping, beneath the mystical Nahanni River, the painting shows Brown lying on one of the oldest rocks found in the Yukon Territory. Painting by Esther Bordet.
Website: www.estherbordetpainting.com
Inside cover photograph credit: by Sarah Chisholm, Brown's winter keeper.

Extreme care has been taken by the author to ensure that all information presented in this book is accurate and up to date at the time of publishing. Neither the author nor the publisher can be held responsible for any errors or omissions. Additionally, neither is any liability assumed for damages resulting from the use of the information contained herein.

All rights reserved. No part of this publication may be reproduced, stored in a retrieval system or transmitted in any form or by any means, electronic, mechanical, photocopying, recording or otherwise without the express written permission of the author.
Contact Maggie Squires at: squires.maggie@gmail.com

Publisher: CCB Publishing
             British Columbia, Canada
             www.ccbpublishing.com

Dedication

A Wild Life And A Dog Called Brown is dedicated to Ted.

"Thanks for the dog, dad. I miss you." - Rose

Contents

ABOUT THIS BOOK ix
PROLOGUE xii
PART I – LIFE BEFORE BROWN
    MOUNTAIN GIRL 3
    FORT NELSON'S PAST 10
    OUR FORT NELSON 15
    UP-THE-HIGHWAY 19
    HIP GIRL GOES WEST 24
    FORT NELSON TO LIARD 31
    AFTER THE BREAKUP 41
    A LOG CABIN AT MUNCHO 45

PART II – LIFE WITH BROWN
    SPRING 2010 – THE PUPPY 53
    SUMMER 2010 – BERRIES, BEARS & BLOOD 62
    FIELD DOG 65
    WINTER 2011/12 – MIN & STEPH 70
    WINTER 2013/14 – BROWN'S BITING HABIT BITES BACK 74
    BROWN'S WINTER KEEPER 77
    BROWN'S PEOPLE 84
    A TRIP TO MUNCHO 90
    BROWN'S LAST DAY 97
    FINAL THOUGHTS 100

ABOUT ROSE COBETT'S GEOLOGICAL RESEARCH 103
ACKNOWLEDGEMENTS 105
ABOUT THE AUTHOR 109

About This Book

When ground that's been frozen since Halloween finally thaws and turns to mud, it's springtime in the north. It was such a springtime, in 2010, when my daughter Rose's dad, Ted Cobbett, asked her to take on the half-Lab puppy that he'd taken to help out a friend but for which he had no time. Rose, that spring, was driving solo the 2,500 kilometres between Vancouver, British Columbia (BC) where she'd been working as a geotechnical engineer, and southern Yukon where she'd be working as a field assistant for the Yukon Geological Survey.

After finishing high school, in 1999, Rose spent the following five falls and winters earning a degree in geological engineering and each respective May-to-October working in the guide-outfitting industry, and then traveled to New Zealand where she spent a year playing rugby. After returning to Canada, she worked for two years with Golder Associates, first in Kamloops and later in Vancouver, and then took a leave of absence from Golder to work as a field assistant for the Yukon Geological Survey. When the Yukon summer work experience was over, Rose knew she wanted a permanent position with the Survey. To be eligible, she needed at least a master's degree, which she didn't have, so in 2009, she returned to the University of BC to get one. Nowhere in this busy life of summers in the field and winters in graduate school was there time to care for a puppy. So, her initial reply to Ted that spring day in 2010 was: "No thanks, dad. I don't much like dogs."

Rose's resistance to taking on a young dog was understandable. As a family, we'd raised no puppies and our experiences with adult dogs had been short-lived and had not ended well. But Ted was persistent, convinced that the puppy's intense gaze meant something special, and he was a darn good salesman. Still, it was only after Rose's younger sister Virginia, who would be at the same northern field station through the summer, offered to help care for the puppy, that Rose relented. The puppy, who she called Brown, never went back to Ted's. A year later, with a master's degree in hand and a permanent position with Yukon Geological Survey, Rose and Brown became Yukoners.

Seven years after adopting her dad's puppy, Ted passed away at the age of 56. Five years later, in 2022, Brown's life was winding down, too. I wondered if the passing of a well-loved dog could hurt just about as much as losing suddenly, and too soon, the dad who had insisted, despite Rose's misgivings, that taking on the puppy he had no time for would work out just fine. So I decided to collect anecdotes and photos from those who had been part of Brown's life and to record the story of Ted and Rose, and of Brown and his people. I asked Rose and her friends, who live a hardy northern outdoor lifestyle and adhere to a hard-work hard-pay philosophy, to share their experiences with Brown. This book is the result of weaving together the stories they shared.

As heartfelt tales about Brown accumulated, the collection of stories begged for more about my childhood and move from North Carolina to Canada, Ted's life in northern BC, our lives together including daughter Rose, and the rugged independence we shared in the Northern Rockies of BC until I left the marriage and the north with four daughters in tow. As a wider story unfolded, I began to reckon with the questions about life that rippled through the tales of Brown and Rose, and among Brown and his people. That is how this collection of stories grew in scope and length.

Part I, *Life Before Brown*, is based on letters and emails that Rose wrote to me as she grew up; recollections that Ted shared about his early life and my experiences and conversations with Ted's family, friends, and acquaintances; and my memories of growing up and decades-ago journey from the southern United Sates (US) to Northern BC. In all of this, there is little to suggest that a dog would end up being a big part of our lives, and especially Rose's. Part II, *Life With Brown*, is the collection of stories shared with me by Rose, and friends of Rose who knew Brown and had loved him well. It includes Ted's passing and also Brown's passing, and reflections about the meaning that Brown brought to our lives.

Prologue

Back in the spring of 2010, in Fort Nelson, BC, Ted handed off to 28-year-old Rose, the second of our four daughters, a puppy he called Buster. At first, though with reluctance, Rose agreed to look after Ted's puppy while she spent three weeks building a log cabin at our Muncho Lake property, located about three hours north of town. But on the return trip to Fort Nelson to drop off borrowed equipment and the dog, Ted convinced Rose to keep the puppy that she had decided to call Brown.

With the puppy reboarded into the front seat of the family truck, a late model Ford F-150 pickup we called the Ol' Grey Dog that Rose had driven from Vancouver, they continued northward. This time, the destination was Kluane Lake Research Station, 260 kilometres west of Whitehorse, Yukon. There, Rose would spend the summer working with the Yukon Geological Survey and collecting data for her master's degree in geology. Virginia, Rose's younger sister, was working at Kluane, too, as the Research Station cook. Midway through a degree in fish and wildlife management, Virginia took the cooking job because it came with the opportunity to assist—in free time between preparing meals and washing dishes—with a study of squirrel behaviour, and to spend time in the wild with her sister Rose.

A few months later, I drove from southwestern BC to southern Yukon to visit Rose and Virginia. Memories of strolling with Virginia down long stretches of sandy shore by Kluane

Lake and catching up with Rose at the end of her long days in the field are intermingled with my first impressions of puppy Brown. On evening walks from the cook shack down to the lake, Brown led the way, and then backtracked to check on each of us. Brown's herding habit and mothering way were easy to warm to. Each of us has cherished memories of that summer by Kluane Lake.

Seven years later, in the spring of 2017, Ted travelled to Whitehorse, as he had every year since 2011, to sell flowers and veggie starts grown in his Fort Nelson greenhouse. After a few years of selling out of a flatbed gooseneck trailer towed behind his Dodge pickup truck, business had grown enough that Ted set up a springtime greenhouse in Whitehorse. From May to June, Rose and partner Nicole handled the business while Ted drove back to Fort Nelson for another load of plants to refill the Whitehorse greenhouse and sell from the trailer as he drove further north to Dawson City and points beyond. The pickup truck, set up with a comfy bed, was Ted's home-away-from-home. Along the route, folks looked forward to buying Ted's exceptional baskets of flowers, grown from seed with great care, and to visiting with a garrulous Ted. Ted loved growing flowers, and travelling and visiting, too.

In the spring of 2017, the set-up changed. Rose and Nicole now had not one but two young boys to care for, the youngest just six months. After helping Ted set up the greenhouse, Rose and Nicole would step back, and Ted's partner would come from Fort Nelson to manage the Whitehorse business while Ted hit the road. On the morning of the day that Ted pulled away and headed for Dawson City, Rose helped load the trailer and water plants and got coffees for the two of them. Helping dad was a break from caring for her young boys and Ted was happy for the extra set of hands.

About forty-five minutes outside of Whitehorse, Ted pulled the trailer load of flowers off the Klondike Highway, stepped out of the pickup truck, walked to the back of the trailer, and collapsed. A passing motorist saw him go down ran over to help but Ted was gone. For our four daughters, the sudden passing of their big-hearted, wild-spirited, free-living dad was a massive blow.

When news of Ted's passing got back to Whitehorse, things rapidly changed. Ted's partner headed back home to Fort Nelson. Rose and Nicole drove the truck and trailer, which had been towed from the highway to a yard in Whitehorse, back to the greenhouse, unloaded flowers, and took over, for one last time, the Whitehorse operation. With their two young boys in tow, Rose and Nicole greeted Ted's friends, spread word of his passing, and shared tears over the loss. The following spring, Ted's partner brought a load of flowers to Whitehorse, but spring was cold and wet and without Ted's enthusiasm for growing and selling, the business wilted and died.

For the past thirty years, Ted and I had lived separate lives. The year before he passed, in the spring of 2016, we both happened to be in Whitehorse and worked together to set up the greenhouse. While the two of us moved baskets of flowers and flats of veggie starts from the trailer to the greenhouse, Ted smoked, sipped whisky, and chatted with customers. As the workday wound down, we grilled steaks and Rose and Nicole brought over potato salad for supper. For that last day with

Ted, I am grateful. There was rekindling of some of the warmth that had drawn us together when Ted was a young man who loved the mountains, and I was a young woman a long way from home and a bit lost, and reminiscing about living in the bush and raising kids together.

During the winter that followed Ted's passing, as Brown slept nearby, a lighter left on a wood stove that was lit on a cold night to warm up the tent, exploded. The accident left Brown prematurely deaf. At seven, already an older dog, the deafness seemed to make his aging more pronounced.

Two years later, when Brown started whining during the night, his indoor bed was moved from inside to an attached garage. At the time, both Rose and Sarah, Brown's wintertime keeper, wondered if Brown's enjoyment of life might be diminishing.

The following spring, Rose departed for what she knew would be her last field season in the mountains with eleven-year-old Brown in tow.

"Brown is the best dog I've known," Rose said. "And the only dog I've known well."

Anticipating Brown's end-of-life, I asked Rose to write about life with Brown. Here is what Rose recorded in her 2021 field notes:

Oh Brown, my mountain companion.

As I approach my fortieth birthday, coming this November, and struggle to accept aging, the wrinkles and especially the grey hair, you inspire me to keep on going, to keep on seeking new adventures and experiences. Once again, you have supported my mountain field work, this time for a Ph.D. Oh, how many rocky miles we've trekked together, and how far I've come in understanding the history of these ancient rocks!

Do you remember how this season started?

On a hot day, you panted for 12 hours straight, walking for much of that long day on bleeding paws that I noticed but you seemed to not notice. Then, at the end of that long day, you collapsed in exhaustion, slept where you laid down (not in my tent)—and did not stir for 24 hours! I thought you might not rise again, that you might pass away in the mountains. A full day later, you rose, to eat, pee, and poo, only to collapse again for another 24 hours. Then, on da three, up you popped, rejuvenated after 48 hours of rest, and day after day, week after week, we did again what we loved doing together, what you and I are built to do. Over the summer, I watched as you slid down steep scree shoots, turned back to find safer routes around cliffs, doggedly climbed mountain after mountain, and arrived at the next station with tail wagging. And, what a welcome surprise that perhaps Sarah's training has finally paid off. You weren't off chasing squirrels, or tempted by a marmot whistle, although it may also be that you no longer hear squirrel chatter and marmot whistles. Hearing well or not, you seem happy, at peace in the mountains. You set the bar high, Brown, and I will aim to keep my mountain-steeped bones wandering Yukon's remote ranges past my prime, as you have, because here I'm at peace, here I have space and time to consider life's complications and still find joy.

I am overwhelmed with emotion and memory.

Some things hurt, like dad's passing away, and the end of my intimate life with Nicole though I hope it's not the end of the two of us as friends and co-parents.

Mostly I feel joy. Joy for so much: my transition from independent mountain woman to mom, housekeeper, chef, and breadwinner; my lasting friendship with Steve, who has been a shepherd in my development into professional geologist, since my first season with the Geological Survey; my bond with my sister Virginia that's grown stronger since we were kids making farts in the wild lands of the Liard River Valley; and, for mom's insistence that we write down the story of life with you, Brown, and for my 40th birthday, commissioned a painting of you in the mountains.

As the 2021 field season and field work for the Ph.D. wound down, I felt tired and unmotivated. It was too muggy, too buggy, and too mossy, things that usually do not bother me and, thus, made me wonder how mountain days without you might feel, and if another dog might follow in your footsteps. Will there be a second Brown who finds the same joy in exertion, physical and mental? You and I have worked together so well in a variety of terrains from steep, rocky peaks with numerous cliffs and rocky scree slopes, to low-lying flats where moss is abundant, the trees and buck brush dense. Brown, you ably navigated terrains of all types, without complaint, except where I had to use both hands and feet to scramble up steep cliffs. When that happened, you barked and whined until you realized I wasn't going to choose an easier route and then back down the mountain you went to search for a dog-suitable route. Brown, you always found a way to climb with four legs the same difficult terrain that I had scrambled up on my own 'all fours,' eventually, sometimes after an hour or two, sometimes staggering from the exertion, catching up with me and rejoining the crew.

Back home in Whitehorse, after our last mountain stint, I felt alarmed and sad with the hard time I had transitioning back to home life and to playing with my two young sons. Are transitions hard because humans crave routine? Feeling alarmed made me try harder to embrace equally all the parts of my life: field work in the mountains; homelife with family; good times with friends; life without dad; whatever life might be without you. I ought to strive, I thought, to weave together life's events and places and people so when loved ones slip away, I can wrap myself with *memories.*

Brown, when you stayed with me for a little while in town before heading back to your winter digs at Sarah's, the extra time helped to remove the inner void I have felt after leaving the mountains and resettling at home: between me and dad since his passing, between me and Nicole when our once-strong bond began to weaken. Both boys loved feeding you, and Sully was almost always up for a walk with you. Nicole seemed at ease when you laid on the front lawn. Neighbours appeared impressed when you seemed content to hoist your aging body into the front seat of the Ol' Grey Dog, where you and I started our life together.

Do you comprehend the subtle sign language that I like to believe had developed between us since your hearing loss? The last trek of this year's field season left me thinking 'yes.' Our final field day was, at last, not so smoking hot. Instead, the day started cold and foggy, and the air didn't warm until late afternoon. That last day, the terrain was easy with soft moss under your healed up paws and almost no brush to scrape your flanks. Ahead of me, you bounded like a fun-loving pup. Periodically, when I peered into the fog, I'd spot you perched, or scouting about, looking majestic in dew-covered whiskers. Brown, you have convinced me that dogs love serving people and that people love dogs as family.

In my studies of the ancient history of a small part of the Cordillera of the Americas, the rocky backbone of mountains stretching from the Aleutian Arc in the Arctic then southward to the Antarctic Peninsula that was birthed over billions of years by the movement of the tectonic plates beneath the Pacific Ocean, I can't help but find analogy with the forces that drive my life.

By mapping rocky outcrops and peering inside tiny crystals to determine formation dates, my studies aim to solve a small piece of earth's space-time puzzle, to help re-enact the slow-moving ancient drama that lifted the Cordillera. My own backbone I lift against steep slopes to explore and map outcrops and collect zircon crystals for dating. My intellect I set to work fitting together the pieces of the space-time geological 'puzzle' to reveal a long gone past. With you, Brown, in my heart awakened a capacity for love and affection, in part, through your dependence on me for food, shelter, and wellbeing. My friend Rory knew firsthand my 'fierce independence' and watched my first steps, with you by my side, towards a life of interdependence with family, partners, and friends.

This letter, written by a daughter who thought, initially, that she was doing her dad a small favour by keeping his puppy for a few weeks, shows the depth of what became a more than decade-long relationship with the dog called Brown. This book explores how the strength of Rose's partnership with Brown grew over time to become a source of confidence and independence, deepen the roots of family, and to draw out unexpected destinies.

A Wild Life And A Dog Called Brown is a tribute to a puppy, adopted with hesitation, who became a faithful, loving, supportive companion to Rose and to his people—a group of strong, independent 'sisters' bonded by a love of the mountains, rugged living, and Brown.

Part I

Life Before Brown

Mountain Girl

Despite living in a rural place, in northeastern BC, where we could've had a dog, where there was plenty of space for both kids and a dog to romp and ramble, dogs weren't part of our life. In that place of boggy flatlands and distant mountains, there were dogs around, for sure, to keep bears away, but we raised no puppies and were not in the habit of having a family dog. Rose's outdoor-focused childhood fostered many interests: sports and fitness, camping and hiking in the mountains, riding horses, cooking over an open fire, and looking for interesting rocks. But not an interest in dogs.

Dogs were mostly absent, too, during my North Carolina childhood. My mother, who was an only child, grew up with a beloved pet terrier. Mom's dad was a professor and the family spent summers at a lovely lakeside cottage where mom and her dog climbed into the boat that was tied up to the dock and rowed together across the lake. Meanwhile, my dad grew up understanding that a dog's purpose in life was to work on the farm and its fate to sleep in the barn.

In my newborn photos, mom's terrier, which came with her to the marriage, appears to be standing guard over my crib. But after we moved, when I was two, to the new house near the outskirts of town, on subdivided land that was once the Sherwood farm, the terrier was gone. There were no further dogs during my growing up years, with one brief exception when I recall there was continual marital strife. Instead, mom's longing for a canine companion and dad's resistance to having a house dog increased in concert. That is until both had grown old, when dad begged for forgiveness and gifted to my mother a Maltipoo, a Maltese-Poodle cross. The small dog named Cricket kept them both in good company.

"I am chief dog-walker within the confines of this campus" wrote dad. "Cricket loves to go out and will bark at anyone he doesn't recognize." On those walks, Cricket dragged along my weakened dad. Of his various mishaps, like peeing on the carpet, dad mostly laughed.

My sister Debby wrote, after mom became ill, "Dad says he will accept the dog bites (dad hugs mom, dog bites dad) and I told him that I would try to orchestrate intimate moments with mom by putting Cricket in another room for short stints. We will see how things go." After mom passed, the dog sought revenge for her absence by biting the only person around, my dad. That's when Debby had Cricket taken away for good.

Ted loved telling stories, but I do not recall any tales about beloved family dogs. If dogs were part of his childhood, they weren't much talked about.

So, when Ted and I got together, it did not naturally occur to us to have a dog or to raise a puppy. Although there were, over the years, a few adult dogs in our lives, none were around for more than a year or two, dying of disease or old age, or simply running off.

So, I suppose you could say, we weren't big on dogs. At least not yet.

Rose, who came along in 1981, was born in Fort Nelson. Heading west from that small town beside the Alaska Highway, after an hour of driving through mostly flat land, the Highway encounters the rolling Foothills of the Northern Rockies that give way to mountain ranges with peaks rising to nearly 3000 metres. As a teenager, Ted scrambled up and down those steep slopes to hunt Stone Sheep and Mountain Goat, and with his brothers boated the many northward flowing rivers to hunt moose and elk.

During her first decade, Rose's summers were spent alongside family exploring the mountains, valleys, rivers and lakes accessible from the Alaska Highway. With Rose, older sister Carolina, and later on with younger sister Virginia, we camped at Kledo Creek, fished at Muncho Lake, and swam in the hot springs by the Liard River. During the winter, when Ted was busy working and often away from home, life was filled with schoolwork, bringing in wood to keep the fire going, and making suppers of caribou cutlets, moose sausage pizza, cabbage rolls, and shepherd's pie.

The year Rose turned ten, I left the north—without Ted. With the girls, all four of them, I moved to BC's Lower Mainland and restarted university. Fifteen years ago, I'd dropped out of school, departed North Carolina, landed in northern BC, and then married and had children. But desire for more education remained. It was a doctoral degree that I wanted, like my dad and granddad had earned, and to succeed in the way that my parent's had expected I would.

After I left the north, the girls spent the school year with me in the Lower Mainland and when summertime rolled around, they headed back to the north to live with Ted. Rose's older sister Carolina decided to live full-time with dad, and much-younger sister Melinda spent summers with me.

At the end of Rose's first year of grade school down south, she wrote in a journal "I can't wait to go north. I really miss the trees and wildflowers."

From up north, Rose wrote to me "I love it here. We ride horses (galloping, jumping logs, taking overnight trips into the mountains), we swim in the river, make campfires on the beach, pick berries, and make jam. One evening on the way back from fishing, we thought we saw frogs jumping in the grass. But they turned out to be mice jumping surprisingly far out into shallow water. I love coming back here, to the mountains. It's a chance to get perspective on life and do some self-reflecting. From time to time, I am humbled, and find that nice, too."

By the time Rose was a teenager, Ted had transitioned from working as a guide-outfitter in the wildlands north of the Liard River to raising buffalo on a ranch outside of Fort Nelson. But Rose was already in love with hunting camp culture, so her summers in the north were spent working for other big game outfitters. In Rose was a burning desire to learn the ropes of guiding and outfitting: cooking in base camp and on the trail, wrangling horses, and guiding the out-of-the-country clients on hunts for sheep, goat and elk. At thirteen, Rose's first camp job was for guide-outfitters Ross and Debby Peck in the vicinity of BC's Tuchodi River. She cleaned cabins and washrooms, did the crew's laundry with an old-fashioned wringer-washer and outdoor clotheslines, and helped with bread-baking, meal prepping, serving, and washing dishes.

"At first, I was not a lot of help but after a few years I had cooking and cleaning at base camp figured out and wanted badly to work outside, not in the kitchen. That wrangling and guiding was considered jobs for males got under my skin. In response, I got fast at kitchen duties and spent my free time outside working with horses, patching gear, and mending fences. I loved the physical challenge of the outdoor work. It was hard, and I loved that it was hard. I wanted to do it all. To cook, wrangle, and guide," Rose told me later.

Packing wooden panniers with basic trail grub, and securing the heavy boxes to a horse's back, Rose practiced standing on a stool that made up for her short height. On top of a thick wool blanket went a wooden pack saddle that was secured with a belly cinch, collar around a horse's breast, and britchen around the hind end and under the tail. When packed with grub and gear, the heavy panniers were hoisted, one at a time, up to the horse's back and fastened to the pack saddle with rope and a diamond hitch. Rose and rope-tying became fast friends. In her free time, she learned how to wrangle stock and lead a string of pack horses safely through mountains and across rivers, to cape moose and elk, and to pack up meat and antlers for the trip back to camp. In short, Rose learned how to guide hunts. So, after a change came in the outfit's management to a less traditional and younger couple with children in 1999, after some further training, Rose was hired as a hunting guide. Finally, she felt equal among her male comrades. When Rose's guide-outfitting days came to an end, she had guided eight hunts: Stone sheep, elk, goat, caribou, and finally, moose.

"Packing food, gear and horses for two weeks on the trail, setting up camp, daily caring for horses, cooking, getting firewood and water, and taking hunters out to look for animals is by far the hardest job I've ever done," Rose told me later.

"I remember feeling a lot of pressure to succeed on these hunts, knowing the world didn't really think women could be hunting guides. I remember feeling super tired, doing tons of physical labour, and getting barely any sleep. You sort of do everything when you are a hunter's guide, and there's a huge element of worrying about someone else's well-being and expectations. Hunting, in contrast, is just about being on the land with the goal of tracking animals."

"The only hunt I really enjoyed was the last one I guided with dad, because we shared the camp work and horse duties, and I was a bit older and managed the pressure a bit better. Though it was still hard work."

"On that last guided hunt when I teamed up with dad, we took out a couple of friends for Muncho Lake outfitters Art and Crystal Thompson. The first day out, my hunter and I got charged by a grizzly bear. The second day out, my hunter shot a record-size caribou. A few days later, when we were out with dad and the other client, my hunter shot a moose. Dad was going to skin the moose for me, but I was firm that I wanted to do it myself. Having never caped a moose, I wanted the experience, so asked dad if he would just help me. He said 'fine' and rode back to camp without helping me at all. It was very difficult to skin the moose and get it packed onto the horses with just me and my hunter. The next day, my body was very sore!"

"It was years before I appreciated that the hard physical work and constant battle with sexism in hunting camps made all the jobs I've had since seem easy" Rose said. "The guide-outfitting experience was special, too, because it left me, after a decade of working in the bush, with lasting friendships."

Fast forward to the spring of 2010. After finishing high school in 1999, Rose completed an undergraduate degree in geological engineering, spent a year playing rugby, two years working as a geotechnical engineer, and finished year 1 of work towards a master's degree in geology. That spring, she felt more than ready for a break from both university and the relentless winter rains of southwestern BC. Rose was more than a little excited to embark on her first research field season up north, in the Yukon, and over the moon about spending the summer in the mountains.

"The mountains are where I feel most like me," Rose declared. "Happy, contented, and grounded."

Rose would drive solo from one extreme end of BC to the other, stopping briefly in Fort Nelson to visit her dad, spend three weeks at Muncho Lake, and then driving further north to Kluane Lake Research Station, in southern Yukon. At Kluane, Rose would spend most of the summer assisting the Yukon Geological Survey with regional mapping, and collecting data for her master's degree.

The route north and up the Alaska Highway took Rose through familiar country: Dawson Creek at Kilometre Zero of the Alaska Highway, the Peace River Valley to Charlie Lake at Kilometre 82.9, and then into Fort Nelson at Kilometre 454.3.

It was midday when Rose pulled into her dad's springtime muddy yard. Anticipating he'd be busy shuffling several irons-in-the-fire, and herself craving to be back in the mountains, Rose intended to have a good but short chin wag with Ted and then head for the hills.

Fort Nelson's Past

Situated east of the Rockies and surrounded by the Interior Plain that stretches across the northeastern corner of BC, the Alaska Highway runs right through Fort Nelson. It takes about an hour of driving to reach the mountains. Ascending the Foothills, the road pitches north and climbs and winds through the Northern Rockies. Deep in mountainous terrain, the Highway follows the eastern shoreline of Muncho Lake and the Trout River, the lake's outflow, down to the Liard River, where the Canadian Rockies end. After crossing the Liard by suspension bridge, the Highway passes by the Liard Hot Springs Provincial Park (at Kilometre 765) and then meanders through the plateaus, valleys, rolling hills, and mountainous terrain of southwestern Yukon.

Thousands of years earlier, groups of Kaska Dene or Denek'éh, a Dene-speaking people, lived throughout the drainage system of the Deh Cho, later named the Mackenzie River, including the area that would become northern BC and southern Yukon. A subgroup of Kaska Dene that migrated southward was probably ancestral to the Slavey people who lived, and still live, in the vicinity of the Nelson River, which was the location of the original Fort Nelson. First Nation camps were located where fish were plentiful: whitefish, trout, grayling, and herring. Seasonally, groups dispersed, crossing rivers by raft, to harvest game including moose, woodland caribou, bear, beaver, fish, rabbits, and duck. When fur traders arrived, beaver, marten, mink, fox, muskrat, and lynx were trapped. Gear, including snares, clubs, bows and arrows, spears, and fishing weirs, was packed by humans and their dogs.

In the summer of 1789, when Alexander Mackenzie explored the Deh Cho, it was renamed it the Mackenzie. Soon after, the fur industry arrived in northwestern Canada. First, Hudson's Bay and then the North West Company established posts, or forts, to trade with First Nations. To trading posts came Roman Catholic and Anglican missionaries, and the Royal Canadian Mounted Police (RCMP) who made regular patrols by boat, horse, and pack train, and snowshoes and dogsled. Trading posts offered guns, twine fish nets, metal traps, canvas tents, and more, and over time, the Dene camps moved closer to them.

For a hundred years, rivers, lakes and overland trails connected a network of remote fur-company trading posts. For example, Lake Athabasca, at the northwest corner of Saskatchewan and northeast corner of Alberta was connected to the post in Fort St. John via the Peace River. The trading post called Fort Nelson, known also as Indian Mountain House, was established in 1805 at Nelson Forks, where the rivers Sahtaneh, Muskwa, Fontas, and Sikanni Chief merge to form the Nelson River. A little north of the Forks, the Nelson River flows into the Liard River, and northward, the Liard joins the Mackenzie, which carries all that water, on the order of 10,000 cubic metres per second, along with a lot of sediment, to its delta on the Beaufort Sea of the Arctic Ocean. As an interesting aside, northerners referred to the direction of river flow as 'down north' because downriver is north. But cheechakos, that is newcomers and non-natives, said 'up north' because maps of the Northern Hemisphere show north at the top of the page. Cheechako comes from 'chee' (new) and 'chako' (to arrive) and was part of the jargon used among traders who didn't speak the same language.

At the Fort Nelson post, there was a church, a store, a house for a priest and a separate house for traders. For a hundred years supplies were delivered by canoe brigade and barge. Then, in 1925, when fur companies finished clearing a 483-kilometre trail between Dawson Creek and Fort Nelson, supplies began to arrive by pack horse and wagon. By the mid-1930's, float planes carrying mail were landing on the Nelson River, and by 1939 those same planes completed an aerial survey of the route that would become the Alaska Highway. By the late-1940's, fur-trade companies were providing decent living quarters and 'messing supplies' including fresh fruits, vegetables, and eggs, so fur traders started bringing their wives to the north.

In 1941, when the US entered World War Two, Canada's northwest was catapulted into modernity. Near the Fort Nelson trading post, the US Army built an airport with building supplies that came from Dawson Creek by tractor train. The new airport served as a refueling stop on the Northwest Staging Route along which hundreds of US war planes were ferried from Edmonton, Alberta, to Fairbanks, Alaska, and then on to Soviet Russia. Originally on the west side of the Nelson River, in 1942, the Fort Nelson trading post was moved to the east side where the overland trail from Dawson Creek was being transformed into the Alaska Highway. With the establishment of modern settlements by the airport, to accommodate the

Canadian Air Force, and by the new Alaska Highway, to accommodate American Army road crews, activity at the original trading post slowed, and eventually it closed for good.

The end of the war with the surrender of the Japanese in September 1945 marked the end of the US Army building boom, but the transformation of Fort Nelson was only just beginning. When the US Army pulled out of Fort Nelson, the Canadian Army took charge of building and maintaining the new Alaska Highway. The Canadian Army moved to the airport where paved roads, a sewer system, running water, and a recreation center, theatre, dance hall, hospital, and store made for relatively easy living. In 1964, when the Canadian Army left and maintenance of the Alaska Highway was transferred to the Department of Public Works, Fort Nelson found new purpose as one of eighteen permanent maintenance camps along the original 2300-kilometre-long Highway route from Dawson Creek, BC to Delta Junction, Alaska.

In the decades that followed the opening of the Highway, Fort Nelson's economy diversified, with much of the development bypassing First Nations. First came the forestry industry. The substantial supply of coniferous and deciduous trees in the Fort Nelson Timber Supply Area supported several sawmills, an Oriented Strand Board, a plywood plant, and a chopstick factory. Industry based on gas and oil boomed next. Gas was first detected in a well drilled for water near the airfield in the early 1940's, and subsequent discovery of the Greater Sierra oil and gas fields led to numerous drilling and fracturing projects. The Westcoast Transmission Company opened a gas processing operation in Fort Nelson in 1964 that was the largest in the western world. The Westcoast plant provided gas to BC's Lower Mainland and the western US through 1288 kilometres of pipeline. Many decades later, when the fracking rush swept through Fort Nelson, a second gas processing plant was constructed but never went into production.

Not unlike many remote resource-based towns, Fort Nelson has boomed and busted more than once. In 2008, the financial crash that began in the US and went on to depress the global economy closed both of Fort Nelson's sawmills and led to loss of more than 400 decent-paying jobs. In 2012, the regionalization of the provincial health care system meant the Fort Nelson Hospital no longer provided maternity care and, in turn, this made the town less attractive to newly minted teachers and nurses looking for first jobs. In 2014, collapse in the price of oil bankrupted the town's major energy sector employer and, in turn, good-paying jobs and the population of Fort Nelson took another blow. While many 'Fort Nellie folks' have made a good living trapping and hunting, building and maintaining the Highway, and in industries associated with oil, gas and forestry, by 2022, the town had been mired in a bust for quite some time.

Our Fort Nelson

In the mid-sixties, when the Canadian Army pulled out of Fort Nelson, Jim Cobbett retired from the service and stayed in the north. When Jim and wife Ruth left army life behind, they had six youngsters, five sons (including Ted) and a daughter.

Retiring from the service meant Jim needed a new job and the family needed a new home. A fine woodworker and skilled handyman, Jim worked at the local hospital doing maintenance, and served as chair of the local Hospital Employees Union.

Back then, fully modernized homes were scarce and occupied by doctors, nurses, teachers, gas-plant managers, and members of the RCMP. Among the available and more modest homes, some lacked modern insulation and were not yet been connected to town water, gas and sewer infrastructure. To those homes, water and fuel came in a barrel that was delivered by truck. Into a just such a home the Cobbett family moved.

But in the still-frontier town of Fort Nelson, there was no shortage of community spirit. Jim was a musician, an accomplished guitar player, and practiced his country guitar licks in a small studio at the back of the house. Along with other music-minded buddies, he formed a band that played at local dances. Ready to hit the dance floor, guys arrived in cowboy boots and gals in winter boots with dancing shoes tucked in a handbag. Couples showed up with a dish of food to contribute to the midnight potluck supper that would be shared by all before the gathering broke up and folks headed back home.

For the growing-up Cobbett boys, there was fishing in lakes

for trout, in streams for grayling, hunting for moose, and trapping fur-bearing animals. In those days, a lynx pelt sold for decent money and the cash helped acquire tracked snow machines. Wild meat, moose and caribou, for example, was a family favourite. The lone sister was tall like her brothers, but unlike the brown-headed boys, was blond-haired. After school and on weekends, she drove the family's station wagon to the highway maintenance camp south of town and tended the convenience store.

More so than his brothers, Ted was full of spit and fire and the spirit of an entrepreneur. He knew how to make folks feel welcome, and dressed the part, too, sporting pink and green western-style shirts made by his mom, Ruth. Over many years, Ted's endeavours to make a living, without bothering to finish high school, included oil-patch contractor, highway construction, big-game guide-outfitter, private pilot, sawmill owner/operator, buffalo rancher, and grower and seller of flowers. In those many pursuits, if Ted was chasing something, I don't know what it was. If he found what he was looking for, I couldn't say. But through all those pursuits, it seems that Ted got through life pretty happily. On the other hand, it's possible, too, that Ted was less happy than I thought he was.

Like Ted's working life, mine was diverse, too. Before leaving North Carolina for somewhere out west, I worked as a nurse's assistant, lifeguard and swim instructor, and on a dairy farm in the Virginia mountains. In Canada, I cooked and waitressed at highway lodges, maintained campgrounds, delivered nature programs at provincial parks, and later on I completed research projects and published journal articles, instructed courses and labs at several Canadian universities, and wrote reports for government and private enterprise. But when I look back at my work life, I don't recall feeling the satisfaction that I think Ted may have experienced. Instead, I recall a strong desire to succeed that was fueled, in large measure, by low self-esteem and lack of self-confidence. Despite dedication and hard work, I never felt rewarded by any kind of career success. It took me a good long while, most of my life I'd say, to understand that enjoyment comes from being part of something, that being kind can be satisfying enough, that contributing what I can to achieving what I sense might be good for all of us can make an endeavour worthwhile. Memoir-writing, including this book, has been healing and helped me put up my head and live well despite all that's happened in my seventy years.

On Salt Spring Island where I spend summers, I am part of a community of boaters, gardeners, and artists. Up north, where I spend winters, I am surrounded by family and write a monthly newsletter for our small, out-of-town neighbourhood. Being part of a small community gives me a measure of self-worth.

Back to the early days of Fort Nelson, the frontier lifestyle of that small-town, nearly 500-kilometres up the Alaska Highway, drew the boisterous Cobbett boys and their competent sister together. She liked to draw and created a collection of family caricatures accompanied by detailed descriptions that poked fun at her brother's bush-life habits. In a series of How-To's, there was How To Dress, Shave & Wash; Tie on Wool Pants; Install & Light a Wood Stove; Prepare Potatoes & Kraft Dinner; and Cook Pancakes & Make Coffee

'*Like a Trapper.*'

"Come and git yer pancakes," Ted loved to say. "Burnt black on the outside and raw in the middle."

'Cowboy coffee' was made by boiling ground coffee then adding a dash of cold water to sink the grounds. "You can teeth-filter the rest of 'em," Ted joked. When the supply of coffee ran low, grounds were boiled twice.

Mom and dad were not excluded from the fun-poking. "Gawd Ruth," cried Jim, "I asked you to hand me the hammer, not hammer my hand."

Before the transfer to Fort Nelson, Jim and Ruth were stationed at the Canadian Military Camp at Chilliwack, BC (where Ted was born), and before Chilliwack, they came west to BC from Ontario. I never heard much said about their lives and families back east though once I met a relative of Ruth's who came west to visit. But neither did I speak much about my own east coast roots. My parents met Ted's parents, once or maybe twice, on RV trips they made from North Carolina to Alaska that took them through Fort Nelson.

Having little to do with eastern relations, I suppose it goes without saying that for us 'family' refers to the 'western branch.'

Up-the-Highway

During the 1970's and '80's, strung out along the 300 kilometres of Highway between Fort Nelson and the Liard Hot Springs, were at least eight off-grid lodges, located every 40 kilometres or so. Some utilized abandoned warehouses, garages, and Quonset huts from the Highway construction days and others were built adjacent to unique landscape features. All were powered by diesel generators, with a back-up to cover down-time when the main engine needed an oil change. For residents of Fort Nelson: Steamboat, Summit Lake, Tetsa River, Toad River, The Village, Rocky Mt., and Circle T Services lodges, plus the four (originally five) businesses at Muncho Lake were collectively referred to as Up-the-Highway. Common among lodges was their remoteness from town, the ruggedness of the surrounding terrain, and the high cost of generating off-grid power. Indeed, the heart of the now-vanished Up-the-Highway community beat to the rhythm of passing motorists accompanied by the drone of a diesel generator.

When a young man like Ted had free time on his hands, he'd spend much of it Up-the-Highway visiting most if not all the roadside lodges between Fort Nelson and the Liard Hot Springs where, for locals, coffee and gossip were served up for free. There might have been a little off-Highway hunting and fishing, too, and for sure a dip in the hot pool.

At the Hot Springs, in the early days of the Highway, a sagging wooden boardwalk led visitors from a small parking lot over the warm water fen, around the warm water swamp, and through the forest to a basic change house and small deck with steps down into a four-foot-deep hot pool formed by a wooden dam at its downstream end. Today, a much-modernized Liard River Hot Springs Provincial Park boasts fifty-three vehicle campsites, a playground and outdoor amphitheatre, new boardwalk supported by rock-filled cages, large change rooms, a full deck, and a second dam below the original one that creates a second shallower and cooler pool below the main hot pool. As locals, we imagined there was no finer experience in the world than a winter dip in the Hot Springs when there were no tourists around, the hot pool was hugged by fog, and trees blanketed with a thick layer of snow and frost bent low over the water.

The 1970's and 80's, about the time that I arrived in the north, were the heyday of the Alaska Highway. RV caravans and bus tours, freight- and fuel-hauling truckers, and adventure seekers from all over the Lower 48 who wanted to see northern Canada and explore Alaska brought enough business to keep open that string of roadside lodges. Back then, driving the narrow, winding, pot-holed gravel road, where washouts were frequent, was a real adventure. The slow but steady march of vehicles kept lodges busy serving meals and pumping gas. The rough condition of the road kept garages busy fixing tires and replacing transmissions, and motel rooms and trailer hook-ups rented while owners of broken-down rigs waited for parts to arrive from 'down south.'

By 1992, the 50th anniversary of the Alaska Highway's 1942 opening, the highway's heyday was over. Fifty years of continuous regrading, rerouting, resurfacing, and straightening of the original Highway, and the improved mileage of more modern vehicles, meant fewer stops, fewer breakdowns and, in turn, fewer customers for Highway businesses. Among the lodges that sprung up soon after the opening of the Highway, those that hung on suffered not only the slow-down in business but the expense of required upgrades to septic fields, water wells, and underground fuel storage tanks, on top of the cost of running a diesel generator. On the upside, the more-or-less continuous Highway upgrading created opportunities for lodge owners to feed and house road crews.

Back in the late 1970's, when Ted and I met by the majestic Muncho Lake that fills a deep valley between the Sentinel and Terminal ranges of the towering Muskwa Mountains, the town of Muncho Lake was composed of lodges, garages, and cabins occupied by road-workers, trappers, hunting guides, outfitters, prospectors, miners, and a Kaska Dena family. Between the south and north end of the Lake there were four businesses: Double G Services, Highland Glen Lodge, Muncho Lake Lodge, and J & H Wilderness Resort. A fifth lodge located across the Highway from the Highland Glen Lodge burned down in 1962. From 1950 until mid-1970, in addition to lodges, outfitting businesses, and the highway maintenance and telecommunications camp, an underground mine was in operation roughly 50 kilometres south of the Lake. Back then, ore was sorted and washed by hand, and the mineralized material, mostly copper, was shipped by road to a smelter southwest of Kamloops. In its heyday, the population of Muncho Lake was forty, up to thirty youngsters in eight grades attended a one-room school, and an old army Quonset hut served as curling rink, dance hall, and movie theatre. The lake-town boom was short-lived.

About the time that activity at the mine was winding down, the unsold lots by the lake that were surveyed for lodges and outfitters became, in 1969, part of Muncho Lake Provincial Park. In 1980, the Department of Public Works relinquished its 99-year lease on land that had been the site of the Highway maintenance camp. As a result, by 1981, the population at Muncho was too low to support the school and it was reopened at Toad River, 55-kilometres to the south where non-park land for development was, back then, relatively plentiful. Of the public services once was located at Muncho, only the Post Office and weather station remained and continued to be part of the operation at Double G.

By 2004, after decades of inactivity, the copper mine's aging roads and infrastructure had been remediated, and much of the land reclaimed for nature. Left behind were the ropes used by the alpine geological team to measure, sample, and map while descending down-mountain. The impressive, glacier-capped Churchill Peak, at 3,202 metres, towers above the cleaned-up mine site. But commercial interest in the copper-rich area has not vanished and junior mining exploration company Fabled Copper Corporation continues to explore the area and report on the potential of the historic Davis Keays and Churchill Copper mine properties, which are closer to Toad River than to Muncho. As the town of Muncho busted, activity at Toad River boomed. From its 1967 start as a trading centre called Toad's River Post near the confluence of the Toad and Racing rivers, by 2022 the town of Toad could boast of a one-room school, a

Highway maintenance camp, a kilometre long runway, and a lodge with gas, café, motel, and campground. Toad River is home, too, to a group of big-game guide-outfitters with hay fields, horses, and pastures, and has a subdivision of rural lots with cabins.

In the late 1970's, Muncho Lake was a thriving Highway town, and when an energetic Ted was free from various work exploits, Up-the-Highway he headed to visit, party, and soak in the Hot Springs. Meanwhile, on a road trip from North Carolina, looking to experience life on the 'other side of the tracks,' I arrived in northern BC.

Hip Girl Goes West

Through twelve years of school, despite troubles at home, with what was probably poor mental health and little time spent studying, I managed to earn mostly 'A's in high school and to get accepted at a decent post secondary institution (the University of North Carolina at Chapel Hill). I started classes in the fall but unlike my high school friends who excelled and went on to become veterinarians, medical doctors, pharmacists, and teachers, I failed to make the transition from home and high school to university. I watched fellow classmates and other first-year students having fun, paying attention in class, and getting good marks, things that I was not experiencing. I enrolled in first-year math, art history, and philosophy but did not succeed in any of them. Instead, I became vaguely aware that something was not 'alright' and was preventing me from concentrating and paying attention in the classroom. Before I failed-out, I decided to drop-out. Rather than head home after dropping out, as my parents insisted I ought to do, I spent the next few years looking for something that would make me feel better and happier.

For a year, I lived and worked on a hippie farm in Rural Retreat, Virginia. Yes, it was a 'rural' farming place. I herded up cows, led them into the corral, and then let three at a time into the milk barn where I inspected and cleaned teats and attached and detached milking machines before letting a cow out to return to the pasture. The early morning and late afternoon tromp through the fields to herd up the Holsteins and lead them back to the milking barn I found immensely pleasurable. The milking process I enjoyed less. When I left the dairy from, I spent time on a commune farm in Ohio, where tomatoes were the main crop. How I found the place, I don't recall. While I was amazed at the volume of vegetables that could be produced in a garden field, more than anything, I felt alone, unsure, vulnerable, disconnected, and homeless. What I thought was being a hippie, wasn't bringing the happiness I longed for.

At some point in all the moving around, I decided I would attend art school. I moved back to North Carolina and, again, was accepted at a university, this time at the University of North Carolina at Greensboro. Wanting to be on my own rather than dependent on my parents for fees and room and board, I worked as a lifeguard at the campus pool and as a waitress at a nearby Pizza Hut. In art class, drawing outdoor scenes with Conte crayon appealed to me, as did combining hand-molded clay shapes with forest objects and bits of patterned fabric to create assembled sculptures. I found rooms in shared housing and to meet the demands of school and work used a speed drug. But after two semesters, once again, I felt lost and disillusioned.

One afternoon, collapsed in misery at the road edge of a paved sidewalk, it occurred to me that the cause of my aimlessness and social self-consciousness was depression, which also plagued my mother. My next thought? If I had learned depression from my mother, then I should be able to unlearn it. But to undo family habits and ways of being, I needed to be away from my family, for a long while. Out of the blue, I decided to go west and homestead. I owned a 1966 Chevy Two (gifted to me by my parents) and had some money saved up. Until I unlearned depression, I planned to have little, maybe nothing to do with my family.

When I told my parents that I was moving across the country, from east to west, my dad firmly said: "Wait a minute. You can't go alone." So, when I pulled out of the driveway of my family's very nice home in an upscale neighbourhood in Winston-Salem, North Carolina with no plan beyond driving westward and homesteading, I was not alone.

So convinced were my parents that it was unsafe for a young, unmarried woman to travel alone, and in need of their support, as I finished my second semester of art school, I looked around campus for someone willing to go west with me. When I posed the question to a guy named Paul, a Viet Nam war vet who was hanging around the university and eating in the cafeteria on borrowed meal tickets (something I started to do, too), he said 'yes' to going west and 'yes' to getting married. And that was all that mattered to me. In a bizarre wedding ceremony in a park, in the company of my parents and my brother and his partner, the two of us got hitched. What I wore, I cannot recall, but Paul was dressed in white and banged on a drum. Looking back, I'm sure my brother was in shock, and my parents scared witless. Back at my parents' home, no one uttered a word as the car was packed with everything they thought we might need, generously provided by my parents. At some point in this wild turn of events, my mother shared with me how much my decision hurt and pleaded with me to change my mind. Mom said something about the blood and sweat she and dad endured to raise me well and send me off to university to pursue a good life. But when she said those words, I was too far 'gone' to listen, never mind reconsider what I saw as my escape from the misery that, at least from my point of view at the time, was the result of my mother's depression.

After the wedding, Paul and I drove to Montana where I got a job in food service. We shared a park campsite with a small group of young people we'd bumped into, a father with a young daughter who had run away from her mother, and a longhaired guy who seemed to be running from everything.

As we drove westward, hour after hour, I noticed for the first time a repetitive jerking on Paul's left side and his thick speech. At the park, which was not a nudist camp, Paul was nude, day in and day out. Pretty quickly, the situation became too much for me. I had no interest in being married, and no interest in getting to know the person whom I had asked to go west with me. I had problems of my own that I wanted, needed, to deal with. I got into the car, alone, and drove toward the Canadian border. About Canada, I knew nothing. I had never heard of the Alaska Highway. I had no passport and did not have a work visa. I drove into a strange country where I knew no one, determined not to contact my family, believing that removing myself from everything familiar was the only way for me to get well. Alaska loomed in the distance, and to Alaska I decided to go.

Somewhere along the Alaska Highway, in the dark, I pitched my tent in a pile of bear shit, and at daybreak discovered the mess. Before tackling the clean-up, I slumped on the grass. Assessing my situation, I visualized myself at the bottom of a deep, dark hole, unable to reach the bottom rung of a ladder. But the top rung was lit by sunlight. I had a decision to make: to give up and drop further into the hole, or to reach up and grab the bottom rung of the ladder. On that bear-shit morning, I resolved to reach up, and to keep on reaching until I emerged into the light.

At twenty-five, I had survived hitchhiking hundreds of miles across the eastern US, when women weren't picked up for nothing. I had nearly flunked out of university, milked cows in the mountains of Virginia, spent a year at art school and a summer on a commune in Ohio, and driven from North Carolina to Canada. Now, more than 1500 kilometres north of the US-Canada border, and 800 kilometres up the Alaska Highway, I was low on cash. My parents would have helped me, but I was resolved to not ask them for help. Instead, I looked for work.

When I drove by the original Highland Glen Lodge located on the shore of Muncho Lake, it was an attractive log building with a huge stone fireplace. It was with a courageous demeanor, which I hoped would mask my vulnerable state, that I went inside and asked for work. The lodge keepers needed help cleaning rooms. They asked no questions. I worked at the lodge until the place closed up for the winter. A few months into the job, the cook looked at me, paused, and then said "Sometimes you look like you are a hundred years old." In that moment, I understood that my journey to wholeness and happiness was going to be a long one.

By the time the Highland Glenn Lodge closed for the winter, a year-round resort at the other end of the lake asked me to be the winter cook. I said 'yes' despite having no restaurant-cooking experience. When winter arrived in that remote, fiercely cold, dark outpost on the Alaska Highway, I knew nothing of forty below and Northern Lights. I was as far from my home in North Carolina, and as out of touch with family and friends as I could ever have imagined I'd be. But that stark, isolated setting in the middle of nowhere seemed to trigger a slow resetting of my view of self and the rest of the world.

During my first cold, northern winter in the late 1970's, in the kitchen of a remote restaurant, I learned to prepare, from scratch, shepherd's pie and rice pudding, dishes I'd never heard of, never mind prepared and eaten. Over the winter, truckers stopped for meals on their way north pulling a load of fuel or freight, and again on their way home pulling an empty trailer. When a trucker complained, in a friendly enough way, I learned to use one knife to chop onions and a different knife to halve toast.

Then, in the middle of my first dark winter in northern Canada, a pair of RCMP officers came into the lodge looking for me and seemed relieved to find me alive. The man I was married to, who shared with me the drive from North Carolina to Montana, was in custody in Alaska for holding two women captive and murdering one of them. The news was shocking and unsettling but, somehow, I managed to carry out my commitment to cook while the lodge owners spent the winter somewhere warmer.

When the owners returned, they needed a waitress for the busy summer season, so I stayed on. Through the summer, there was a steady stream of American travel trailers looking for hook-ups and tour-bus passengers looking for lunch. When the highway was quiet, I took note of the small group of local guys who came Up-the-Highway on days off from the oil patch and highway maintenance crews, looking for a party and a dip in the Liard Hot Springs.

In patched-up jeans, T-shirt, long braids, and sneakers, maybe I was attractive in in some new way, or maybe I was someone to conquer. At some point, I understood that among these local boys, Ted among them, there were bets about who would be the first to 'bed' the American woman. In cowboy boots and hat, Ted was a full foot taller than my not quite five-foot frame. Alone in a strange new place, a little attention from a spirited young man was impossible to ignore. At some point, Ted borrowed a couple of horses from Otto Amundson at Muncho Lake Outfitters and invited me to ride out to Trapper Arnie's lakeside cabin to do some moose hunting. Well, Ted got a moose, and got me, too. What did I get? I got hooked on the idea of living in wild places. Eventually, I got unmarried from Paul (by an annulment arranged and paid for by my father), and Ted and I married. Within a few years, with two kids in tow, we moved to a remote cabin by the Liard River. I was thrilled with the opportunity to learn something about homesteading.

Fort Nelson to Liard

Between 1979 and 1990, our four babies were born, all girls, and all delivered at Fort Nelson's full-service general hospital. In spring of '83, when we uprooted from Fort Nelson and headed off to live in the bush by the Liard River, I was pregnant with Virginia, baby #3, who arrived just before the end of June. Before we left Fort Nelson, baby #2, Rose, was toddling well enough to navigate, proudly without big sister Carolina alongside, up and down the short side street where we lived in the original Cobbett home. Up-the-Highway, down-river, and north, Ted would be a big-game guide-outfitter for the Wildlife Management Area that stretched from the north side of the Liard River to BC's border with Northwest Territory.

Like the Trout River that flows out of Muncho Lake, the Nelson River runs into the Liard. In turn, the Liard discharges into the mighty MacKenzie or Deh Cho, which flows all the way to the Arctic's Beaufort Sea. Peering into the future, in the 1990's, I would spend eight summers as a graduate student in the Northwest Territories' town of Inuvik, situated on the eastern edge of the Mackenzie River's expansive, lake-rich Delta. But back in 1983, with two kids and a third 'in the oven,' Ted and I homesteaded on a wide-open bench above the Liard, eleven kilometres downriver from the Highway suspension bridge that crosses the river. After driving across the bridge, just before passing by the entrance to the Liard River Hot Springs Provincial Park, a dirt path veers in and out of a wide ditch and then disappears into the forest. This unmaintained bush road runs parallel to the river, tracks through forest, crosses creeks, and rounds a bend before climbing a modest slope to our treeless bench. Off to the right, stood the cabin that Ted built for pregnant Maggie, three and a half-year-old Carolina, and eighteen-month-old Rose. From a modernish home in town with running water, lights, and heat we moved into an off-grid log cabin in the middle of nowhere. Within a year, there was a dirt air strip, too, where Ted landed and took-off in the Super Cub he'd learned to fly. Getting hunters and gear to far-flung cabins was a lot faster in the Cub than on horseback. The Cub was s a taildragger designed to take off and land in a short distance. Having the Cub meant guides trailed horses in and out of bush camps at the beginning and end of hunting season rather than guides and their hunters making the long ride, as was the case in our first season or two.

The cabin was built with logs harvested from a 1982 burn that scorched the bark and killed, but left standing, a decent-sized stand of white spruce. For the cabin, logs were installed vertically. A barn-like second floor and tin roof completed our new home. Inside, along the middle of the front wall were stairs that led to a two-sided loft. At one end of the loft were beds for kids, and at the other end a bed for parents and the new baby. In between the two loft bedrooms was a gap that opened to the main floor below.

On the main floor there was a wood stove for heating the place. On cold mornings, it was tough to get out from under the blankets piled high to stay warm through the night. When the fire was going, I sat facing the stove until its heat filled the room and warmed my back side, too. On winter days when a cold north wind blew down the Liard Valley, the only warm place was no further than a foot from the wood stove.

Ted liked to say: "We've got air conditioning in the winter and heating in the summer."

As we lay in our beds, wolves howled in the wild. Inside, wild mice that succeeded in burrowing in between the bottom of a vertical log and the cabin floorboard would, without warning, nip at the hair on any head that wasn't completely buried beneath a pile of bed covers. I surmised that the mice must be collecting material for nesting in this newly discovered warm spot in an otherwise cold forest. The night-time hair-nipping led me to regularly use a flat screwdriver to shove bits of insulation between log butts and the floor to keep mice out.

Cooking, for the first few years, was performed using a wood cook stove, and after that with a restaurant style propane range with two big ovens and an expansive grill. From scratch and a sourdough pot, I made loaves of brown bread, English muffins, bagels, and cinnamon buns. I loved baking at home, and still do! I learned, too, how to cut, wrap, fry, roast, and stew wild meat.

When the propane stove was moved in, the wood cook stove was moved to the porch and used for canning. On the porch, too, was a hand grinder for processing wild meat, and a hand mill for grinding grain. In the front yard stood a hand-operated washer and wringer alongside a clothesline. Hung outside year-round, laundry sun-dried in the summer and freeze-dried in the winter.

Within a year or so, there were add-ons: a dining room for

serving meals to hunters, and a smaller room to support a water reservoir that was a repurposed fuel tank. In the spring, the tank was filled using a gas-powered pump that delivered spring water from below the house up to the roof. All summer, force of gravity provided running water into the kitchen sink and into a toilet. Both the sink and toilet discharged over the bank, downstream from the spring. During the winter, when the external water tank was unusable due to sub-zero temperatures, we collected snow in metal buckets for melting on the woodstove. At night a bucket came upstairs and was carried back down each morning and emptied into the outhouse.

From our perch on the bench above the river, we enjoyed a wide-open view of the Liard Valley. There was plenty of room and soon enough there was a garden, a cluster of hunter's cabins, an airstrip, a couple of sheds, a horse corral, a chicken coop, and later a pig pen.

Although the cabin was only eleven kilometres from the Highway, to a trio of little kids, it must have felt like the middle of nowhere. To Rose, who was walking well enough to self-navigate up and down our small-town street in Fort Nelson where neighbours kept an eye out and brought her home if she wandered too far, the Liard homestead was a place of lost freedom. She wailed by the door when we wouldn't let her out to walk about on her own.

To compensate for the loss of walking freedom, we built a sandbox beside the cabin, just outside a big side-window, where we hoped Rose would feel free to play while we kept an eye on her. Indeed, Rose seemed contented out there until late one afternoon, when we looked out and she was neither in the sandbox nor in the yard by the house and didn't answer when we called her name. As daylight faded, we started to worry that we'd need outside help. But on one last walk down the dusty road, Ted heard a cry from the bushes on the far side. What dad said to little Rose I didn't hear. One way or another he read Rose the 'riot act' and she did not again wander down the road and off into the tall grass.

Instead, Rose began to watch out for other opportunities to exercise independence. One afternoon, while the rest of us were planting potatoes beside the creek, Rose vanished. We didn't worry much until we were ready to head home and then, in a panic, searched the stream and the trail above and below it. No Rose. I hurried off towards home while the rest of the crew took one last look around the garden patch before heading home, too. At home, I found Rose asleep on the couch. When dinner was made, Rose came to the table and dozed off, we thought, until dessert was served. Rose got pretty good at her 'sleep through dinner and wake up for dessert' ruse until we finally caught on and put an end to it.

Most of the year, getting from the cabin to the Highway down the unmaintained bush road was a slog. When the road was dry, it took a half-hour by truck. But when the road was springtime soggy or wintertime snowy, the trip took the better part of an hour by three-wheel all terrain vehicle, feeling the bumps on the butt, or by snowmobile feeling the cold in fingers and toes. Behind the skidoo, the girls snuggled in a blanketed sled. On the three-wheeler, they held on tight to the front and back racks. If we flew in the Super Cub, which was rare, the trip took a few minutes after taking off from the front yard, flying upriver, and landing on the Highway. In the back of the Super Cub, the girls sat on milk crates. During the summer, along with the girls, I travelled daily by three-wheel bike to the Hot Springs Park where I worked at one job or another: maintenance contractor, wood provider, and naturalist - which was the park job I loved best!

With money earned working at the park, we bought five-acres of land at Muncho, on a hill above the lake, where the burned-out lodge was stood. Perched on a flat spot halfway up the hill was a skid shack where a younger Ted spent time with 'Uncle' Arnie and Arnie's friend Loren, who used the place as a base camp for hunting and trapping. From Arnie and Loren, and later on from Muncho Lake outfitter Otto, Ted learned to be a hunting guide.

At Muncho, we felt connected to community, and it was easy to get there by truck or plane. In addition to working at the Liard Park, I worked at Muncho's two provincial campgrounds.

Ted and I both stayed busy, so it didn't matter much to me that he was away from home most of the time. After all, my dad had been away from home a lot. After putting in full days at the research lab (his Ph.D. was in microbiology), dad spent evenings and weekends participating in local politics, starting up a music store, or in the basement workshop or garage repairing appliances, cars, and musical instruments.

During service in WWII, in the US Army Air Force, dad was similarly busy fixing things. At the end of a regular shift, he headed off the base to work at the local telegraph Express Agency. At the base, with a hand sewing kit, he made extra money fixing basketballs, hats, boots, and patching clothing for fellow service men. At one point, he asked his folks to send out a sewing machine so that he could alter clothing, too. With buddies, used cars were bought, fixed up, used for sightseeing and to get to off-base jobs, then sold for a profit. During the war, when radios and alarm clocks were scarce, dad and his buddies bought, fixed up, and resold used ones for a small profit, too.

Dad's habitual fixing of stuff got its start during his boyhood. During the Great Depression that followed the stock market crash of 1929, when dad was seven, his family uprooted from a comfortable house in town, where his dad was a chiropractor, and lived in an old hearse that his dad converted into a traveling home. They lived on various family homesteads until the Depression wound down and jobs were once again available. After the family returned to town living, dad finished high school and one year in college before he was drafted. During the near decade long Depression, his family raised animals and gardened, and hunted for small game. For cash, they picked crops and sold fruit. To save money, trips to town for bulk supplies were in a vehicle shared with neighbours. Dad's particular contribution was resizing and resoling the family's shoes using scrap leather and rubber- a habit he never quite left behind.

When we were kids, my dad taught my younger brother Tom to fix all kinds of things. The same opportunity was not extended to me. Though I yearned to spend time with my dad, doing so seemed to me to make my mother unhappy. Instead, I latched on to opportunities to hang out with my brother. Some of those bro-time memories, like playing base ball in the front yard and hooking up a light bulb to a battery and switch, remain crystal clear to me.

In Ted's case, guide-outfitting meant being away from home almost year-round. Spring and fall were hunting seasons, summers were filled with building and maintaining bush cabins, air strips, equipment and trails. Winters were spent state-side to book new hunters. Being away from home was Ted's opportunity to party, too. Although I wanted more time than I got with my dad, I felt alright having a mostly absent husband. I was happy to be self-sufficient.

In contrast with garrulous Ted, I kept to myself. Being alone felt safe. After all, my mother was a homebody who loved sewing clothes and drapes for the house, bow ties for her husband, and knitting sweaters for all of us. At my cabin home, I stayed busy with laundry and cooking, organizing grocery orders and supplies, and during the hunting season, with cooking for hunters as well as family. At the park, I cleaned campgrounds, led nature walks, and gave evening talks, all while trying to keep an eye on the playground where the girls were spending days and early evenings.

But it was quiet moments in the forest that I enjoyed most. Among trees, blended with nature, and in the face of bouts of furious weather, my body and mind became one. At Liard, joyful moments outdoors sustained me and provided an antidote to the depression that came along when I left North Carolina. Even so, I continued to believe that I'd learned depression from my mother, and that I could unlearn it by being far from my birth family, staying busy, working hard, and being outdoors.

Busy with our individual lives, things began to change between Ted and I, at first not so noticeably, but much more so when an unplanned baby arrived, seven years after Virginia, our third, was born. One afternoon when the park was unusually quiet, a single visitor showed up for the afternoon nature walk. We walked anyway, just the two of us. Instead of identifying plants and birds, my walking buddy shared with me that in her work she helped folks with addictions. Somewhere along the path we stopped, sat on a log, and I spilled my fears about Ted's drinking and lack of financial responsibility. From my companion that day, I came away understanding two things: first, the two problems, drinking and financial irresponsibility, were probably linked; and second, there was nothing I could do to fix either of them. For the first time in more than a decade of marriage, I allowed myself to look at and to share with someone the situation I was in with Ted. It was also the first time that I understood, at least in a vague way, that I was unable to face the situation that I was in and to find a way to work with it, or through it. After all, I had no previous experience with making a marriage challenged by alcoholism and debt work. In addition, I lacked any understanding of and had no tools to help myself with depression.

Near the end of our marriage, I received a letter from my dad expressing concern about my well-being. It broke me open. After an agonizing six months of 'do I go?' or 'do I stay?' I left both the marriage and the north. In 1990, with a new baby in tow, I headed to southwestern BC, to re-start university. Going back to school felt, in a way, like a reconnection with my family roots, where doctors of various disciplines appeared on both sides of my family tree.

Looking back, though, my ten years in northern Canada and, in particular, my time spent living at Muncho Lake and Liard, was a halcyon decade, a time of relatively idyllic happiness. I can still feel the excitement of my first trip to a wilderness camp, and of my first inkling of what living 'in the bush' was all about. The transformation that started that first cold, dark winter at Muncho Lake, continued when Ted introduced me to 'living in the bush.' When I left the north, I took a love of wild places, of being physically engaged with living simply among rocks and trees, and water and sky along with me. And, I knew I'd go north again.

After the Breakup

After Ted and I split and I moved south, Ted continued to outfit at Liard, and the Muncho property became mine. The three older siblings were happy to spend summers with dad in the wild lands of northern BC. Perhaps they got the best of both worlds: winters in southwestern BC filled with playing rugby and field hockey, participating in ballet class and jazz band, going to birthday parties and on picnics, and much more; and summers in northeastern BC, filled with fishing in creeks, flying in planes and helicopters, trailing horses into remote hunting camps, sneaking up in the dark on elk that slipped silently into an open horse corral to lick salt blocks, among other 'bush' adventures. Later on, at Ted's ranch in Fort Nelson, there were chickens to feed, goats to milk, and a tractor to drive.

During summers with dad, the girls got more of his attention, I think, than during the times when we all lived together. The rest of the year, the girls got too little attention from a busy student-mom. While making dinner, I read, while taking a bath, I reviewed notes. As I pursued one degree after another, the girls got less and less from me.

One day Rose said to me, "Mom, all the other parents come to watch games. I want you to watch my games, too."

So, I started to attend rugby games and track meets, band concerts and school plays. But I was short-fused, too, and as a result, the girls were often walking-on-eggshells. When I said 'yes' to an opportunity to do research in Canada's western

Arctic, recalling the richness of my experiences in northern BC, it made my daughter's lives even more challenging.

This time I landed further north than the Liard River in northern BC, to the Mackenzie River close to where it flowed into the Arctic Ocean. At Inuvik, where I was stationed, the lake-rich delta of the Mackenzie River stretched westward for 80 kilometres, and from south to north was over 200 kilometres long. As the Mackenzie, or Deh Cho, approaches the Arctic Ocean, water flow slows and, in turn, sediment picked up from the mountains of northern BC and southern Yukon is deposited to create one of the most extensive and lake-rich deltas in the world. I would end up, over eight summers, studying how the frequency of flooding of river water into delta lakes, which ranged from less-than-annually to continuously, affected gradients of water transparency, chemistry, and productivity. There not much about the research experience that I did not deeply appreciate.

The arctic research experience differed in many ways from the Liard outfitting experience. For one thing, I was alone. To keep family out of mind, I worked long hours in the field and in the lab. It was easy to get up early and stay up late in a place where the sun was up night and day. The used bicycle I bought to get around town, with a child seat that was handy for hauling groceries, allowed me to explore the river from one end of town to the other. For exercise, and to keep my head clear, I regularly cycled part of the Dempster Highway between Inuvik and the local airport.

The town of Inuvik, like Liard and Muncho and even Fort Nelson, was surrounded by forested wilderness, where I felt safe, and at home. At the time, the 'highway' north of Inuvik to the Arctic Coast was the river, traveled during open-water season by boat, and when frozen, by vehicle on the ice road. Since 2017, 15 years or so after I left Inuvik for the last time, an all-season road has connected Inuvik and the Arctic coast town of Tuktoyaktuk. When my graduate research wound down, on my last flight from Inuvik back to Vancouver, I knew with certainty a chunk of my heart would be forever frozen in arctic ice, just as I knew I'd feel forever warmed by Liard Hot Springs. I knew my inner pace of life would forever abide by the rhythm of the lakeside community that once thrived beside the 223-metre deep glacial-green mountain lake called Muncho, beneath the sky reaching glacial-white Churchill Peak.

By the time I was finished with university with a doctorate degree and post-doctoral experience, three of my daughters were resettled in northern Canada, within driving distance of Muncho Lake and Liard Hot Springs. And within a few years, my fourth daughter would move north too.

Rose finished high school, where she excelled in sports and math, in 1999, and then matriculated at the University of British Columbia in geological engineering. She knew she was a mountain girl. Grounded among rocks, sure-footed in steep terrain, and mountain-fit, Rose's true home was in the rocky hills that rose sharply from Muncho's stony shoreline, and in the white and black spruce covered slopes that rose gently from the Liard's incised valley.

Rose's connection to Muncho Lake started at her birth, in 1981, when she was named after a Kaska Dena woman, Theresa Rose MacDonald, or Rose. Theresa Rose grew up in the bush not far from Muncho Lake. The McDonald family lived in the wilderness surrounding Muncho Lake from around 1900 until the last of the siblings passed away in 2000. The family made a living by hunting, trapping, and guiding moose hunts. Theresa Rose and her sisters Elsie and Lucy cut and dried moose meat over an open fire, and tanned moose hides by hand using moose brains. Then, with the softened, wood-smoked hide, they sewed mitts, moccasins, and mukluks.

When I first arrived in northern Canada in the late 1970's, while doing lodge work at Muncho, I met the McDonald family, visited their Moose Lake camp, and from sisters Lucy, who was outgoing, and Rose, who was a quiet homebody, I learned about hide tanning, and sewing mukluks and moccasins. With Lucy I walked from the Highway to the family's Moose Lake camp. Ahead of me, carrying a heavy pack and wearing moccasins, Lucy walked without pause through forest and stream. Not daring to complain about my wet feet, I followed along in silence. When we reached the shore of Moose Lake, Lucy made a smoky fire to signal to her older brother Walter. Across the lake he came, in a small aluminum boat powered by an outboard motor, to pick us up. My daughter Rose, like Lucy's sister Rose, is a sewer of mitts, moccasins, and mukluks that she decorates with beads and the fur of animals trapped in the north. Self-taught, Rose got better at hide-sewing with practice. Like Rose McDonald before her, Rose Cobbett is most at home in the forest.

A Log Cabin at Muncho

In the spring of 2010, when Rose drove to the Yukon from Vancouver to undertake field work for the research component of her master's degree in geology, her plan was to spend three weeks at Muncho to begin work on a new cabin that to replace the old skid shack.

Since 1942, when the Alaska Highway was opened to public travel, continuous upgrading steadily modernized the road connecting Dawson Creek, BC and Delta Junction, Alaska. By 2010, much of the Highway was widened and straightened, and flanked by broad, grassy rights-of-way, the kind that can make driving monotonous. But an hour north of Fort Nelson and right up to Muncho Lake, much of the modern Highway still followed the original route through the Rocky Mountains. Flanked by canyons and waterfalls and hugged by forest, the Highway crossed and recrossed wild rivers, and moose, caribou, Stone sheep, mountain goat, and black bear might step out of the forest and cross the road ahead of any vehicle.

Muncho Lake's glacial-green water fills a mile-wide mountain valley that stretches for 12 kilometres. Along its southeastern shore, the Highway right-of-way was blasted out of bedrock, leaving water lapping at one edge of the road and steep cliffs rising from the other. Near the north end of the lake, where the Lakeview Lodge burned down in 1962, was the five acre plot of land we purchased years ago. Now surrounded by park land on both sides, in the 1940's the Lakeview Lodge occupied three five-acre lots and provided fuel, food, and lodging to Alaska Highway travelers. Today, all that remains of the lodge is a pair of gas pumps embedded in a concrete slab. Unless, that is, one walks from the Highway to the bulldozed pile of burnt debris at the back of the property. There, among encroaching poplars, under a thin veneer of dirt and moss, it is possible, still, to unearth old car parts, rusty pots, and odd bits of weathered, rusty metal. Even a license plate from the forties has been added to the collection of old stuff carted uphill to the clearing by the old skid shack.

Getting to the property from the Highway still means driving through the ditch. Getting to the clearing halfway up the hill rising steeply to the south, still means crossing the rubble-filled flat where the lodge buildings once stood, and then driving up a steep, rutted, grown-in driveway. The skid shack, pulled up the hill and tucked up against the treed slope some fifty years ago to serve as Uncle Arnie's trapper cabin, was to us a beloved second home. By 2010, however, the old place was badly weathered and over three weeks, while camping in the shack, Rose intended to start building a new cabin. The new building would be built of logs and sit in the shadow of Muncho's forested hills and rocky peaks and overlook the lake.

Rose was keen to build a log cabin because her bush-kid roots and mountain-childhood mattered more to her than anything else in life. University degrees mattered too, but in a different way. Training and education in geology, and research in the ancient history of the mountains of Canada's western Cordillera provided Rose with a way to make a living doing what she loves: being in the mountains. Building a log cabin provided Rose a way to stay in touch with her growing-up-in-the-mountains roots, her namesake Kaska Dena 'sister,' the slopes her dad once hiked to hunt sheep and goat, and the place her mom and dad met. Perhaps of even greater importance was a strong desire to prove to herself that she was as strong and capable of building a log cabin as any young man might be.

A friend of Ted's felled the trees that would become the new Muncho cabin, trucked the logs north on a flatbed trailer, and offloaded them at the bottom of the hill by the Highway. The previous spring, in 2009, the log-peeling was completed, thanks to several weeks of hard work by Rose, her friend Rory and his twin brother Liam. Wanting to experience the north, the brothers were happy to hang out at Muncho and peel logs for a few weeks. Rose peeled, too, and cooked for the three of them.

The following year, 2010, Rose planned to work solo. Using Ted's picker, which was mounted onto a pickup truck, she'd move each log uphill and build walls one log at a time. Rose was committed, eager, and ready to learn by doing. During the three weeks, with a little greenhorn luck, Rose hoped to install footings and lay the first or a few round(s) of logs. Between moving and placing a log, was the important step of scribing, or carving, the shape of each underlying log into the overlying one. A well-scribed groove guided the shape and depth of the saddle notch at each end and ensured each log snuggled up to the next. The groove determined wall thickness, too, and allowed moisture to escape as stacked logs dried. To cut notches and grooves, Rose used the chainsaw that Ted gave the girls at Christmas. To hollow out the grooves, she purchased a curved chisel and an adze. Rose was determined to build a cabin of well-fitted logs.

"For three weeks straight, each day ended with aching shoulders and sore hands, arms, and back. But the soreness didn't dampen my spirit. Each morning, I got up ready for another long, hard day of cabin-building," recalled Rose.

By the end of the third week, Rose was convinced she could build a cabin by hand. By the time the log walls were finished, she figured she'd be pretty good at using a chainsaw, chisel, and adze to carve grooves and cut saddle notches. Learning by doing required more than hard physical labour though. It was an education, too, in understanding the 'best practices' of cabin-building. Despite knowing first-hand that keeping out the cold air that settles in during long, dark northern winters means building an airtight cabin, when someone asked Rose what she was using for insulation between logs, her reply was "Nothing." Soon after, from an old book on cabin-building, Rose learned that insulating the groove between logs was as important as carving logs to lay snuggly against each other.

Before asbestos, which from 1952 to 1992 was mined north of Muncho, at the Cassiar Asbestos Mine, and well before the manufacture of Fibreglass insulation, moss was the standard insulation in log cabins. Rose was thrilled to use natural insulation despite reading that moss could shrink and fall out as it dried. From the hill behind the shack, Rose gathered the fluffy moss that grew beneath lichened white and black spruce trees. A large amount of moss was easy to collect and haul by hand to the cabin site. Back at the cabin, fighting self-doubt,

Rose disassembled five rounds, one log at a time and then surged with pride as she filled grooves with moist moss, end-to-end, and replaced the logs. Because Rose was doing a decent job of grooving and notching, the log fit was snug, and finishing with moss was a labour of love.

It would take Rose a few more short summer and fall stints to finish the cabin walls, and then with help from friends and her dad, add a loft and deck, and put on the roof. After completing the cabin, several more years passed before the greatest outcome of Rose's inexperience in cabin-building became evident. At some point, the packrats that naturally inhabit this part of the north managed to tunnel in between the roof and the log walls. The nuisance packrat is the Bushy Tailed Woodrat *Neotoma cinerea* with an intimidating tail-to-snout length of 30-centimetres. Although its range extends into southern Yukon, we've never seen it anywhere but Muncho. Fixing the problem could mean removing the roof, which is a job for an experienced crew.

Until it is fully rat-proofed, by one means or another, the sturdy new cabin, built by Rose with help from her friends and dad, with a roomy well-lit loft, a tin roof that doesn't leak, and an airtight wood stove, won't get a lot of overnight use. In the meantime, it's a great cabin for daytime activities with a view of the lake out front and view of mountains out back. There's plenty of firewood stacked outside. Inside there's a propane stove along with basic food and cooking supplies stored in a rat-proof cupboard. Out front, there's a wide, covered deck beside a fire pit.

Packrats aside, standing alongside the old shack, the new log cabin by Muncho Lake is a place where family gathers. The home place at Liard is gone, and there are new owners running that guide-outfitting business. But at Muncho, roots put down over time have grown a sturdy family tree: a mom with four strong-willed and hard-working daughters, four energetic grandsons and, in 2022, a new granddaughter. The old shack and new cabin are full of memories: snowy winters and warm fires, cold skidoo rides and hot spring swims, lake ice and pond hockey, berry-picking and jam-making, and summer camping and hiking.

When cabin-building started back in 2010, none of us could ever have imagined that a dog would soon transform our lives

Part II

Life With Brown

A Wild Life And A Dog Called Brown

Spring 2010 – The Puppy

There were two reasons for Rose's decision to cabin-build alone at Muncho. She wanted to know that she could work as hard and as well as any other young man or woman. For too many hunting seasons she'd been told 'how to,' shown 'how to' or told 'you can't' do what the male hands did, including cabin-building using hand tools. Rose was strong and fit, especially after a winter of playing university rugby. She wanted to be challenged, she didn't want to be helped, or want the work to be easy.

Rose possessed a fierce desire to be independent. Rory, Rose's good friend and former beau during their university years, observed on their many adventures, and not always with enthusiasm, Rose's fierce drive to succeed under her own power. In Canada, they paddled and biked to the Pitt River hot springs; cycled across Southern Gulf Island's Galiano, Pender, and Texada; canoed from Tagish Lake to Whitehorse; hiked, climbed, and paddled at Muncho; and visited many hot springs and old mines by car, foot, and bike. Further afield, they cycled in the Chilean mountains and in the Bahamas, and toured Peru.

Looking back, "Rory's keen interest in planning and executing our next adventure was the glue that kept the relationship going," Rose told me. "Eventually, when I took a job in White- horse and started looking ahead to having a family, the two of us drifted apart."

Of her strong desire and drive for independence Rose said, "I was quite young, I think, when I learned to take care of my own needs and wants and found that being independent was the easiest way to ensure that I was content and getting what I needed out of life."

In spring 2010, this time on a solo adventure, Rose drove from Vancouver to Fort Nelson, then from Fort Nelson to Muncho Lake for a three-week stint, then back to Fort Nelson and north, again, to Whitehorse and Kluane Lake Research Station. But as it turned out, during the three-weeks at Muncho, Rose was not quite alone. At the stop in Fort Nelson to visit her dad, Ted introduced her to a dog called Buster. Buster was a decent looking puppy, less than a year old, blackish with tinges of brown, and one-half Labrador. When Rose pulled into Ted's place, Buster was tied to a post next to a doghouse in the middle of his muddy yard. Springtime in the north is called break-up, fall is referred to as freeze-up, and after the ground's been frozen all winter, springtime is gum-boot season.

"Buster's line was so tangled that he could just barely avoid sitting in his own poop, and it was impossible for him to get into the doghouse and out of the mud," Rose told me later.

Feeling a twinge of sadness for the pup, Rose thought to herself, 'Come on, Dad.'

After a few smokes (Ted, that is) and a good chin wag, it was nearly noon. To get to Muncho and settled in before dark, Rose needed to hit the road.

As the two of them transferred gear from the Ol' Grey Dog to the picker-rigged truck, Ted said to Rose, "Take Buster with you. He needs to get out of the yard."

"Yes," Rose muttered under her breath, "Buster needs to get out of the yard" but quickly said aloud: "No thanks, dad. I don't much like dogs."

Ted pressed. "Then just take him for a few weeks. He's really a good dog, better than many I've come across."

Despite mixed feelings about taking care of dad's dog for the three weeks she would be at Muncho, Rose relented. Ted untied and handed over Buster, Rose shoved the puppy into the front seat of the truck, Ted tossed the sack of dog food behind the seat, and Rose resettled behind the wheel. With a wave, Rose and Buster rolled down Ted's driveway, back onto the Highway, and headed north to spend three weeks at the Muncho property. In Ted's yard, the Ol' Grey Dog would sit until Rose returned, switched trucks, dropped off Buster, and then continued the drive north through Whitehorse and out to Kluane.

About halfway into the three-hour drive from Fort Nelson to Muncho, Rose pulled off at Summit Lake, inside Stone Mountain Park. At 1,295 metres, Summit Lake is the highest point on the Alaska Highway. Nearby, a cold-water creek offers to quench the thirst of travellers, and a short, steep trail a chance to stretch cramped-from-driving legs. After Rose and the dog piled out of the truck, Buster surprised Rose by running wildly about with a gleeful look in his eyes, overjoyed, it seemed, to be out of the pen, out of the truck, and outside in the middle of nowhere. Buster plunged into the water and sprinted around and around like a racehorse. Rose, unable to stop laughing, was unexpectedly impressed with this high-spirited pup, and happy that Buster was along for the drive.

"Is it possible I could like a dog, that I might like this dog?" Rose wondered.

Moments later, her excitement faded to worry that Buster might not come back to the truck. Again, Rose was pleasantly surprised. After some convincing, Buster scrambled back to the truck and snuggled into the front seat for the rest of the ride. Back on to the Highway they rolled.

The next stop was Muncho Lake. At Kilometre 707 Rose pulled off the Highway, drove through the ditch, crossed the flat, and then drove the back side of the hill to the cabin site. So close to the Highway, it seemed risky to let Buster run about. Instead, the two of them headed inside to get settled in the old skid shack, where they would stay for the next three weeks.

Many years ago, Arnie transformed the square skid shack into a cozy home. A few internal walls created a small room off the kitchen with a back door and a dresser; a bigger front room with a wood stove, fold-out couch, and single-pane windows facing north, and an L-shaped kitchen. At the short end of the L, there was a wood cook-stove that smoked like heck when first lit and then worked like a charm for cooking and baking. Against the wall were shelves that could be sealed up with a hinged board and two front legs that allowed the shutter to drop down and serve as a counter. Down the long end of the L was a small table and chairs for eating, with more windows. Between the cook stove and the table stood a counter with a sink and drainboard, and a pair of windows looking east.

By the small table, a doorway led to a closed-in porch, used for gear, with a sink for washing up. The porch led to an enclosed mudroom with a door to the outside. Out of the mudroom door was a well-traveled path up to the outhouse, skipped downhill, Buster's barks were the first sounds she'd heard from Ted's dog.

Back at the shack after her run, when Rose peered through the front window to check on the pup, she was in for another surprise. Buster had crawled into the sleeping bag that she'd left rolled out on the foldout couch.

"He looked comfortable as heck with his head resting on his front paws and the rest of his body tucked into my cozy bag. I felt like he crawled into my sleeping bag to spite me."

Her next thought? "A dog that's smart enough to figure out how to get into my sleeping bag might be a dog I can like, and the name Buster doesn't at all fit."

The pup seemed too smart to be called a name that conjured a dog along for the ride, a prankster not to be taken seriously. Rose decided to call the puppy Brown and felt justified in doing so because at the time, Buster was a dark brown dog. Later on, after treatment for worms with a little Copenhagen snuff, the pup's brown hairs were shed and, in their place, grew in a shiny black coat. At this point, the name Brown didn't work so well, but it stuck.

As days turned into weeks, Rose sensed that Brown was listening and responding to her and, in turn, she let him trot alongside when she crossed the Highway to get water, go for a run, and use the lodge payphone. But one afternoon, walking across the lodge parking lot, Brown lunged aggressively at a small dog on a leash. Quickly, the older couple pulled their little dog up close and a safe distance from Brown, but said nothing.

"Ugh," Rose said quietly, mostly to herself. Embarrassed and remorseful, she delivered a hard slam that sent Brown to the ground and hoped he'd gotten the message that his behavior was not ok. Licking her wounds, Rose walked Brown back to the cabin and returned to the lodge, without him, to make the phone call.

Within a few days, Rose regained enough confidence to allow Brown outside while she worked in the yard. But behave Brown did not, bolting off after a wolf. Despite the wolf's nonchalant reaction to Brown's barking and charging, Rose wondered if she'd seen the last of the pup. But no. Soon enough, Brown came sauntering back, alone.

"Maybe not quite soon enough," Rose thought aloud, "Brown will be back at dad's."

Thinking that her time with Brown was temporary, Rose had no inkling that Brown's pranks at Muncho foreshadowed events that, years down the road, would profoundly alter Brown's life, and hers, too.

Three weeks later, her cabin-building time used up, Rose drove back to Fort Nelson to return the truck and the dog to her dad, and then continue northward in the Ol' Grey Dog. Rose had warmed up to Brown but was happy and relieved to drop him off back at dad's place. Doing a master's degree at a university down south and spending summers and early falls up north, she told herself, was all she could juggle at once.

But Ted had a different idea. As Rose packed up and prepared to roll, once again, down dad's driveway and up the Highway, Ted did his best to convince Rose to take Brown. "It will all work out just fine," he insisted.

While mulling over her dad's plea, Rose called sister Virginia, who'd be spending the summer, too, at the Kluane

Lake Research Station.

"Would you help me take care of a dog?"

"Of course," Virginia replied.

So, wondering how life with a dog could possibly work out just fine, Rose and Brown climbed back into the Ol' Grey Dog for the drive to Whitehorse at Kilometre 1425, then onto Haines Junction and Kluane National Park at Kilometre 1579.

Virginia, the Research Station cook, was happy to help look after Brown. During days in the field, Rose worked at training Brown to be her field assistant, to hike alongside, and to be the lookout for bears. In the evenings, when food prep and dishes were done, Virginia would take Brown to the lakeside cabin as both companion and bear-dog. In midsummer, when I drove north to Kluane to visit Rose and Virginia, it was easy to warm up to the dog called Brown as he herded the three of us between the cook shack and the lakeside cabin.

As the field season wound down, Rose confessed that Ted had been right. That first summer with Brown, the summer of 2010, though not without incident, had worked out just fine.

Summer 2010 – Berries, Bears & Blood

Kluane is Yukon's largest lake and nearby Kluane National Park and Preserve is home to numerous and equally, if not more, spectacular features: Canada's highest peak, the nearly 6000-metre-high Mount Logan; the world's largest and longest non-polar ice field; vast tracts of tundra and forest; wild rivers; and wildlife including wolves, lynx, mountain goat, Dall sheep, moose, and grizzly bears. Mountains and glaciers make up more than eighty percent of the Park's terrain.

Between the top of Kluane Park's mountain peaks and its valley bottoms, the sharp elevational gradient corresponds with striking changes in geology, climate, and ecology that provide opportunities to study a range of topics including the history of mountain-building, and how climate change may affect glaciers, plant, and animal communities. In 1961, the Arctic Institute of North America established a Research Station beside Kluane Lake, at the base of the Saint Elias Mountains that dominate the National Park. Over sixty years later, the Institute continues to support studies in glaciology, zoology, geomorphology, and climatology, among others.

Virginia worked as the Kluane Lake Research Station cook in 2009, and she was back to cook again in 2010, this time with sister Rose and the puppy, Brown. Cabins for visiting researchers were located close to the runway, kitchen, meeting rooms, and laundry facilities, as well as down by the lake. Along with the rest of the Yukon Geological Survey crew, Rose put up her tent just off the airstrip. Virginia, after long days of cooking for up to eighty people, preferred the quiet of the lakeside cabins that were located a short walk from the camp kitchen. By the lake, there was room for the small greenhouse that Virginia built from odds and ends of wood and plastic, to grow up veggie starts she'd brought up from Ted's commercial greenhouse in Fort Nelson.

Brown spent days with Rose in the field, and nights with Virginia in her lakeside cabin. In the morning, before Virginia reported for kitchen duty, and before Rose and Brown took off for the mountains, the three of them walked together along the lakeshore.

In the sandy loess-based soil Among the lakeshore cabins, grew thick stands of *Shepherdia canadensis*, commonly called soapberry or soopolallie. The loess was derived from rocks ground down by glaciers and, being flour-light, was easily picked up and carried downwind. The perennial *Shepherdia* rooted easily in the light soil and reached heights of over two metres. *Shepherdia* is dioecious (with male and female flowers on separate bushes) and by mid-to-late summer, on the female bushes there was an abundance of fuzzy red berries. Edible but bittersweet, the so-called soapberries appeal not so much to humans but hugely to the grizzly bears that inhabit Kluane Park's lush alpine meadows and valleys. When soapberries ripen, in July and August, grizzly bears forage for the fruit along the Kluane lakeshore.

Bears in the vicinity of camp, especially from mid- to late summer, meant Brown was not the only dog at the Research Station. The Research Station managers had a dog named Dove, trained to stay close to their young daughter, Bronwyn.

Dove stayed on Bronwyn's heels to ensure her safety, especially when bears were around camp. On her own down at the lake, Virginia was nervous about bears, especially during soapberry season. Having Brown with her at night, growling when bears were nearby, made it easier for Virginia to get a good night's sleep and wake rested for her early morning kitchen shift.

But, as it turned out, bears were not the only danger Virginia encountered during her second summer at Kluane. On Canada Day, the camp hosted a celebration that drew friends and their dogs from nearby Haines Junction and Whitehorse for an overnight stay at the lake. After a big dinner, everyone, along with the dogs, headed down to the beach to play a game of touch rugby. The dogs were initially in a playful mood, but when a friendly dogfight escalated to neck biting, Virginia became fearful that a still-young Brown might suffer worse than a hearty pummeling. In a few quick moves, Virginia reached in and yanked Brown's tail. Just as quickly, Brown turned and sunk his teeth into Virginia's hand.

When the dogfight wound down, Virginia, not Brown, was injured and bleeding. Virginia, headed off to the nursing station in the nearby town of Haines Junction for a tetanus shot and bandaging. The next morning, she was back in the kitchen but with a hand the size of a baseball and an ego bruised by knowing the fault for the injury was her own. The mishap was traumatizing, and left Virginia with a lasting fear of dog fights.

Field Dog

When the 2010 field season at Kluane was over, and the work for the Yukon Geological Survey was completed, Rose felt lucky to pick up a short-term contract with a small prospecting company with an office in Whitehorse.

"Three of us plus Brown flew around southeast Yukon and stopped to look at various target areas. After we landed and got out of the helicopter, each of us hiked for a few hours in a different direction. Brown would start out with me and then take off for a while but always rejoin me before it was time to get back in the helicopter and head to the next stop. I never waited for him. This was the first time I realized what an amazing field dog Brown was going to be. "

With writing the master's thesis looming, Rose decided to spend the winter of 2010/11 in Whitehorse, with Brown. When that winter wound down, the two of them had house-hopped among three locations: a house-share in Whitehorse; a farm-sit south of Whitehorse in Atlin, BC; and a room rental in a Whitehorse subdivision. Each time they moved, Brown's doghouse and bale of hay moved, too. Despite all the moving around, the thesis got written, and in the spring of 2011, Rose returned to Vancouver, defended her thesis, bought a station wagon, cleared out her Vancouver apartment, and moved to Whitehorse—for good.

By summer of 2011—not (yet) successful landing a permanent position with the Yukon Geological Survey—Rose was thrilled with get another contract offer this time to map for junior mineral exploration company Archer, Cathro & Associates. But company rule number one was 'no dogs in camp.' Right away, Rose let the company know she would not do field work without Brown, a well-behaved dog, she claimed. No longer a puppy, grown-up Brown was loyal, obedient, a little goofy, and independent (with a mind of his own when it came to chasing wild animals). Faults aside, after the previous summer's field experiences, Rose knew with certainty that Brown would spend every field season by her side.

Rose waited to hear back that, after all, she would not be working for Archer Cathro because bringing along the dog was a deal-breaker. But she didn't hear back, and when it was time to go, Rose and Brown flew together into camp. During the flight, Brown appeared carefree. Rose was worried. Seated next to Brown, Rose dreaded the reception she might face when a dog followed her out of the aircraft. The half-hour flight from Whitehorse to camp was in a Skyvan, nick-named the 'Flying Shoebox' because of its boxy shape. The plane was a twin-propped turbo with a 20-metre wingspan and enough room for 19 passengers and gear. After the plane landed, Rose and Brown disembarked, Rose grabbed her gear, and the two of them headed straight to base camp and settled in their tent.

With the company boss expected in camp the next day, Rose remained worried. She'd heard the boss described as both 'down to earth' and 'all business.' The next day, as soon as the boss deplaned, Brown bounded over, sat on his boss's foot, leaned in for a snuggle, and let out a loud fart. A moment of trying to not laugh out loud faded quickly to embarrassment and then to anxiety about what might come next. But the boss said nothing.

In camp, Brown was on 24-hour bear duty. Brown's sharp ears, eyes, and nose were as highly valued—maybe more even—than Rose's mapping expertise. When Brown cut his paws on sharp rocks and spent a day in camp to heal up, the whole crew fell in love with his quiet manner, kindred spirit, and attentive ways. After two five-week shifts in the mountains, Brown was well-liked and the entire Archer Cathro gang was sorry to see him go. Looking back, Rose figured that Brown's strong sense of duty and his ease with people made for easy bonding with her campmates.

Rose's confidence in Brown grew, too. Though off and running after small and big game, Brown behaved differently around bears. One afternoon, ready to head back after hiking up a ridge to look at a cliff face, fifty metres below them, a grizzly bear was eating berries. Uncertain if Brown would give chase, Rose said quietly and firmly, "Brown, sit." He obeyed instantly. In silence, the two of them watched, and after ten minutes or so, the bear retreated downslope. When the bear disappeared from sight, Rose started down and Brown stayed right by her side.

The following summer, of 2012, Rose was hired again to map for Archer Cathro. Brown, the bear dog, was welcomed back, too. This time, Rose made moose-hide booties to protect Brown's paws on long traverses over rocky terrain, and canvas panniers so Brown could serve as Rose's rock hauler. Brown didn't much like the booties, but the load of heavy rock samples on his back he did not seem to notice.

Whether it was fondness for Brown or high regard for

Rose's mapping expertise or a combination of both, the field work for Archer Cathro was a success. Rose came away from the three short term mapping contracts convinced that Brown would be part of every field season, even if there was a field assistant, instead of Brown, to haul rocks. Looking back over a full decade of field seasons, Rose's prediction proved to be right. Every summer, in every camp, Brown performed very well as Rose's field assistant and was a beloved camp dog, too.

The display of infectious energy by the puppy Brown back in spring of 2010, on the drive to Muncho in the Ol' Grey Dog to spend three weeks cabin building, when he plunged into the creek and ran a few racehorse laps, became a seasonal ritual of Brown's. At the start of each field season in the mountains, as soon as Brown disembarked the plane or helicopter that delivered him alongside Rose to camp, off went Brown to run a few fast laps. Each time the energetic display brought a smile to her face.

Indeed, Rose admitted, "Brown's willingness to get in beside me—whether in a truck, plane, or helicopter—was one of his most endearing qualities."

By 2021, Brown had put in eleven summers of mountain field work, all but one with Rose, when she was too pregnant to go. During this time, he thrived as comrade, protector and trail-finder and loved the freedom to roam in the wildlands.

"It should not surprise me," Rose mused, "that my campmates loved Brown almost or as much as I did. In the field, Brown would start and end each field day with me. In between, while field work kept me preoccupied, I didn't worry when Brown disappeared for an hour or two or a few, or when he returned tired out. He always re-joined me before we got picked up by helicopter for the flight back to camp. One evening, when the crew regathered for supper, each crew member mentioned having seen Brown at different times throughout the day. It was then that I figured out what Brown was up to during long absences. He was checking on each crew member, and sometimes that meant covering an enormous distance on his own."

Winter 2011/12 – Min & Steph

At one of Rose's house-hops during the thesis-writing winter, she lived briefly with Min and Steph. Steph, from Vancouver, was in Whitehorse to get practical experience in social work. She leased a house and rented out a few of its rooms. Rose rented one of them. When Min arrived in Whitehorse from Australia, seeking a northern adventure, he too rented a room from Steph. Not long after Min moved in, Rose moved out and went to work for Archer Cathro.

Meanwhile, Min and Steph hit it off as a couple. Min was slightly built, goofy and serious in equal measure, with a big smile hiding beneath his ginger beard. Steph, with waves of brown hair framing hazel eyes, could not hide her warm heart. Min and Steph moved out of the leased house and into a cozy cabin on Lake Laberge, outside of Whitehorse, and soon after they were pregnant.

After finishing her first mapping contract with Archer Cathro, Rose fell into her own romance with Nicole. Rose and Nicole met the previous winter when both played hockey in the Whitehorse women's league. Nicole, and her small Yorkie-Chihuahua named Abby, moved to Whitehorse from southern Alberta to learn carpentry from a family friend, Ray. Abby, who could almost fit in the palm of a hand, had belonged to Nicole's mom, who had passed away suddenly, a few years earlier. After her mom's passing, Nicole and little Abby were inseparable. Ray, who has known Nicole pretty much her whole life, moved to Whitehorse a few years before her. Working with

Ray, Nicole discovered a passion for woodworking and, in turn, enrolled in a furniture-making course in Scotland. At the end of the 2011 field season, Rose and Nicole flew together across the North Atlantic. Abby stayed with a close friend of Nicole's. Brown spent the winter with Min and Steph at the rental cabin on Lake Laberge.

An hour or so north of Whitehorse, Lake Laberge is not really a lake but a two to five kilometre wide and fifty-kilometre-long section of the Yukon River. Flanked by the Teslin Mountains to the east and Miners Range to the west, it's a beautiful and inspiring location. Min regularly skied on the lake and attempted to skijor with Brown. Skijoring combines the power of skiing and poling with the strength of a dog, or dogs, running and pulling. Both skier and dog wear a harness and are connected by a leash or length of rope with a quick release so they can easily disconnect. Skijoring can be a fast, thrilling way to travel across snow or ice, but a dog must be trained to pull, and to follow the human voice giving directions, as there are no reins to control the puller, or mechanical devices to signal a change in direction. Brown was strong and fast, but skijoring was a game of Russian Roulette. Whenever they headed downhill, if Brown saw a squirrel, off the trail he went. Each time, Brown's sudden change in direction left Min faceplanted in the snow.

"He couldn't get over those bloody squirrels," Min recalled later.

Despite Brown's hapless first attempt, within a few years, Brown would become a very fine skijor dog indeed.

When winter ice gave way to summer open water, Min and

Brown went on a week-long car trip to Fort Smith in the Northwest Territories. During the day they drove, and at night they slept in the car.

"Sitting up front, Brown seemed surprisingly content," Min remembered, "He garnered considerable attention from both locals and tourists. At night, he didn't complain about serving as my pillow, comforter, and heater."

Min and Steph had their own dog, too, called 'Brown Dog.'

"Brown and Brown Dog could not have been more different." Min explained, "Brown was a lively, charismatic, affectionate, attractive and playful two-year-old. Brown Dog was a geriatric, demented, and chronically depressed mutt with several rapidly growing tumors. Yet, despite these obvious differences, the two forged a strong bond."

In the spring of 2012, as soon as Rose and Nicole returned from Scotland and were resettled in Whitehorse, they went to pick up Brown, looking forward to having him home, too. They were in for a bit of a surprise: Rose had left a sack of dog food and instructed Min to feed Brown two to four cups a day. For scooping out dry dog food, she placed a large yoghurt container inside the sack. Dutifully, each day, Min fed Brown three yoghurt tubs or nine cups of food! When Rose and Nicole picked up Brown, he was no longer a lean dog.

Following Brown's winter and spring at Lake Laberge with Min and Steph, in the summer of 2012, Rose and Brown did another stint of mapping for Archer Cathro. Then, finally, before winter fully settled, Rose was offered and accepted a full-time job with the Yukon Geological Survey. With permanent employment secured, Rose and Nicole quickly made plans to add kids to their family of two women and two dogs, Brown and Abby.

Within a few years, Min returned to Australia along with Steph and their new family where he started medical school. At some point during Min's long stretch of training, they started to miss Whitehorse and Steph's family in Vancouver. With three kids in tow, Min and Steph returned to Canada for an extended visit and spent a good chunk of it in Whitehorse where, in 2019, Min and Brown enjoyed a memorable reunion.

Winter 2013/14 – Brown's Biting Habit Bites Back

After Rose and Nicole returned from Scotland, they lived part-time in a tiny cabin on Ray's acreage and part-time in a wall-tent with a wood stove at their acreage up the Klondike Highway, near Lake Lebarge. In the winter of 2013/14, they purchased a condo in the south end of Whitehorse. Brown was well-loved. Nicole and Abby were inseparable. Rose struggled to accept Abby's defensive growling.

To step out of the back door of the condo into a forest of trails suitable for skiing, hiking, walking, running, and cycling, and where Brown was free to run, seemed perfect. Until, that is, Brown bit a small dog and kept on running. Immediately, an ad was broadcast on the local radio station by the owners of the injured small dog, seeking to locate the culprit. Word got back quickly to Rose and Nicole that Brown was 'wanted.' With deep regret, Rose and Nicole called the owners of the wounded dog, apologized as well as they could, and paid the vet bill. Next, they faced a new reality for Brown. The town biting incident changed everything.

During the summers of field work in the mountains with Rose, Brown was free to chase and kill small game with impunity. Now, it seemed impossible to train a grown-up dog to not chase small animals, including dogs being walked in the forests surrounding Whitehorse. Knowing Brown could unpredictably harm not only small game but small pets, too, he was muzzled when he went along for skis, walks, and runs.

Brown did not like the muzzle. Worse, Rose and Nicole could sense the fear folks felt when they passed by a muzzled Brown. It was a sad turn of events when Brown was no longer free to run unmuzzled through the forest.

Rose decided to ask out-of-town friends if any might want to keep Brown between the end of each summer field season and the start of the next one. When someone highly suitable stepped forward, they felt lucky, indeed. Brown's new winter digs would be in Haines Junction, a small-town about a 1.5-hour drive west of Whitehorse.

Each summer, at the start of the field season, Brown would reunite with Rose, and they would spend the summer together in the mountains. Rose would map, and Brown would look out for bears and wolves, chase small game, and keep an eye on the field crew. At the end of each field season, when snow in the high-country spread downslope and forced the field crew to retreat, Brown would retreat, too, to Haines Junction, where he was well loved by his winter-keeper(s): first Sarah, then Sarah and Jeffrey, then Sarah, Jeffrey, and their children Abel and Clare.

In early 2014, Rose and Nicole's first son, Sawyer, arrived. Their newborn got lots of attention from Rose and Nicole, and Brown, too. Abby remained defensive, and Rose's impatience with the little dog did not diminish. Rose spent the following summer at home with baby Sawyer, and Brown went to the field with Esther, a workmate of Rose's. In the fall, Brown moved to Haines Junction to live with Sarah. After Brown's move, it wasn't long until Abby, too, left the condo and went to live with one of Nicole's sisters.

When all was said and done, living part-time with Brown worked out just fine. But Nicole missed having Abby by her side.

Brown's Winter Keeper

Sarah grew up in Nova Scotia in the company of two older brothers and a dog. After earning a degree in Resource Management, Sarah spent a decade working in remote parks and field camps in far-flung places like Hawaii, Antarctica, and the Canadian Arctic. By 2014, Sarah was over thirty, and the appeal of adventure travel and working in exotic places was fading. In its place was a new dream: settling down and having a home and a dog of her own.

When a job offer came from Kluane National Park and Preserve, near Haines Junction and Sarah said 'yes,' she figured she might be there for a while. There was no inkling, at the time, that Haines Junction would become, in her words, "And, I don't think I'm overstretching here, my forever home."

In the search for a place to live in Haines Junction, Sarah asked a prospective landlord if dogs were allowed in the rental house.

The reply, "Well, you can't live in Yukon Territory without a dog" fed Sarah's suspicion that Yukon just might be a good fit for her.

Sarah grew up with a well-loved mutt called Tim and knew that one day she'd have a dog of her own. During the globetrotting of her post university life, Sarah filled the dog void in various ways. She borrowed dogs, volunteered to dog sit and, in Nunavut, cared for a team of Inuit sled dogs.

Sarah's first season at Kluane as a Park Resource Management Officer was the busiest summer she'd ever experienced.

Budget cuts that reduced summer staff from ten to four meant long days and frequent seven-day work weeks. Sarah's working days were filled with training, monitoring, managing, and rescuing injured and lost visitors. This very busy first season at Kluane suggested to Sarah that, at least during the summer, she'd be living in Yukon without a dog. It was not possible to have a dog and spend so much time working in a park that doesn't allow dogs.

When her neighbour Georgie approached Sarah about a fit, adventuresome dog called Brown with a summer job but in need of a winter home, it seemed too good to be true. Sarah jumped at the chance. First, she arranged to take Brown for a trial weekend in Haines Junction. Then, Sarah worried that Rose and Nicole might be uncomfortable when Brown took off with a stranger. When she arrived at the Whitehorse condo, she was relieved to find that Rose and Nicole were relieved, too, that she was interested in becoming Brown's winter keeper. For his part, Brown jumped into the back of Sarah's car, without hesitation, and settled in for the drive back to Haines Junction. When Sarah stopped to stretch her legs, Brown bounded out of the car and stretched his legs, too.

"Brown's relaxed manner and tuned-in response spoke loudly that he was a pretty good dog," Sarah told me later.

By day two, Sarah knew Brown was a keeper.

Inside he was calm and well-behaved. Outside he was ready to go and highly energetic. Brown would disappear into the bush but also keep an eye on Sarah. She was relaxed, knowing that Brown was looking out for her, and watching out, too, for wildlife both big and small.

"A perfect wild-forest companion, Brown was for me," Sarah decided.

About a year later, Sarah bought and camperized, a right-side driver mini van so she could travel with Brown, during the spring and fall, to music festivals, campgrounds, beaches, and pullouts in Yukon and Alaska. Drawing the line at having Brown in her bed, Sarah loved the mornings when she awoke to find Brown curled up in his front seat, looking out the window. Of course, Brown's seat was on the left side of the van, usually the driver's side, and that meant a lot of double looks when the two of them pulled up at stoplights. Sarah swears that Brown acquired the habit of looking both ways when the van pulled up at stop signs.

Having Brown from fall through to spring, meant that Brown was Sarah's winter ski buddy. Sarah found Brown to be more like a tank built for endurance than a racehorse built for speed. With crystal clarity, Sarah recalls the moment she realized that Brown was nothing like the wild sled dogs, the huskies, that she trained in Nunavut. Running a team of wild dogs meant coming around a corner and, not infrequently, heading straight into a cold stream. Stopping a team of sled dogs was impossible. With Brown, after grabbing the quick release and yelling, "Whoa, whoa, whoa," he would stop and look back to see what Sarah wanted.

"What a revelation!" Sarah thought. "A dog that wants to work with me and not just satisfy some inner racehorse drive!"

Over time, Sarah found it interesting, even intriguing, how Brown reacted to his 'people.' Among Sarah's circle of friends and acquaintances, a reciprocal connection to Brown's stoic, calm energy, and warm response to petting was either instant or absent. With Brown's people, the connection was instant, and, in turn, there were many requests to take him along for an afternoon or weekend adventure. Often, in some soft way, Brown would reciprocate his good fortune by helping someone through heartache or assisting parents by romping with their kids. Once, Sarah watched Brown, in a sweet, gentle manner, help a toddler overcome fear of dogs. Brown took a leaf gently from the small hand that offered it, then dropped it, which led to a giggle, and a repeat of the leaf exchange, as the small child became increasingly relaxed around the big black dog.

When Sarah first met Jeffrey, who'd grown up in the small Vuntut Gwitch'in village of Old Crow, he'd recently returned to the north after studying Resource Management and accepting work at Kluane National Park. Quiet, gentle, and bush-wise, Jeffrey became Sarah's partner, and Jeffrey's dog Niija, a young poodle mix, became Brown's best buddy. Niija's youthful goading and pawing kept Brown acting younger than his age.

One winter, Jeffrey and Sarah took off with the dogs to spend a month living in Sarah's van and travelling to various hot springs to ski and swim. Niija and Brown loved touring together. During the day, the dogs snoozed while Sarah and Jeffrey shared the driving. At night, the dogs moved up front and hunkered down in their custom doggy bench and Jeffrey and Sarah climbed into the back of the van where they stretched out for the night. But two weeks into the trip, both dogs got worms and living together in the van stopped being cozy. In Fort Nelson, they picked up a deworming remedy but somehow got the wrong medication and endured, in that small, shared living space, two weeks of worms crawling across the dog beds.

"Ugh," Sarah said about the last half of that trip with two wormy dogs.

Skijoring was Sarah's favourite way to travel across the land, and many splendid skijoring adventures were shared among Sarah, Jeffrey and the two dogs. A few of them were especially memorable. At the Halfway Hot Springs, near Nelson, BC, the four of them skijored the 17 kilometres from the highway to the hot pool. Other park visitors were making the trek, too, but with two dogs happy to pull two humans on skis, Jeffrey and Sarah sailed past those who were slogging through wet snow on snowshoes and skis, or bogged down and digging out four-wheel drives. After skijoring in and soaking in the hot water, the four of them were well on their way back before the others even reached the hot pools.

"That was a smug moment," recalled Sarah.

Friends, and also a few strangers, occasionally referred to Brown as Sarah's 'baby' or to Sarah as Brown's 'mom.' But the relationship, for Sarah—and for Brown, too, she thinks—was more like a partnership.

"We took care of each other, and each of us took the relationship seriously."

Another time, Jeffrey and Sarah joined friends Lloyd and Andrea on a ski out to a cabin at Granite Lake, near Haines Junction. It was a full-day ski with the dogs pulling pulks (small sleds rigged with a harness for pulling) that were loaded with supplies. The weekend was colder than they anticipated, with temperatures dipping to -35/-40 degrees Celsius, but they went anyway. The dogs were troopers pulling pulks the whole way with only a few short rests. On the return trip, Brown pulled Sarah on skis, and Sarah pulled the pulk. Heading down a slope, the sled hit a tree, and the sudden pull back threw Sarah to the ground. As she got up, there was a wave of pain that became excruciating when she stood. With five kilometres to go, Sarah was unable to ski. Not wanting to make a big deal out of the pain, shuffling along as well as she could, Brown strained to pull the combined weight of Sarah and the pulk. That day, Brown was more hero than partner and Sarah was awash with gratitude for Brown's strength, work ethic, and determination.

Throughout both of Sarah's two pregnancies, Brown pulled more than his share of the weight. It was important to Sarah to stay active while pregnant, and she continued to go on long-distance ski trips despite feeling less confident in her strength and energy reserves. But with Brown along, Sarah knew, if needed, that she could hook up to Brown and he would pull her, an expectant mom with a big belly, back home without overexertion. Again and again, Sarah was grateful for Brown's strength, obliging nature, and capacity to adapt to their changed, more dependent, relationship.

After Sarah and Jeffrey's first baby, son Abel, arrived, their relationship with Brown changed again. No longer an adventuresome unit of two humans plus two dogs, a third tiny human altered the pace of life, especially outdoors. Yet Brown adapted, leaving Sarah and Jeffrey free to focus on their new son as they walked together through the woods. Later, when Abel was a toddler, Brown, again, adapted, showing patience with and responding gently to Abel's pokes and prods. Once again, Sarah was filled with gratitude for Brown's patience, presence, easy-going nature, and willingness to match the pace of meandering toddler-directed wood-walks.

"I never heard Abel laugh as excitedly and gleefully as when Brown entertained his advances and played with him in the yard, grabbing his stick or getting excited and running hot laps around the house," Sarah shared.

"I think Brown might be a once-in-a-lifetime dog, though he was not without faults. We had our share of unnecessarily rough attacks on other dogs. I will say to his credit they were mostly annoying dogs but, in my view, that does not excuse Brown's worst habit. And I am less tolerant than Rose may have been, at least in the beginning, of Brown's habit of killing and eating small game. Oh, and there were those loud smelly farts that occurred at the worst possible times, too often in the presence of respected, easily disgusted visitors, or on long, stuffy car rides," sighed Sarah.

"Bad habits aside, Brown will be impossible to replace," Sarah shared.

"I cannot imagine another dog so loyal, so adaptable, so able to be whatever his human companions need him to be."

One more thing needs to be said. Brown drew people together, and through Rose and Sarah's co-ownership, a small group of humans who loved Brown began to refer themselves as Brown's people. Not everyone who met Brown loved Brown, but those who felt connected to Brown also felt connected to each other.

Brown's People

One moderately cold day in November 2020, a small group met at a forest pond outside of Haines Junction to skate on hallowed ice—that magical kind of ice that occurs when it's been cold enough for thick ice to form but not warm enough for the first big snowfall. Sarah came from Haines Junction with newborn Clare, bundled into a buggy, son Abel, husband Jeffrey, and Brown. Rose and I came from Whitehorse with her sons Sawyer and Sullivan. Stephanie came from Takhini with her son's Connor and Thomas. Each of us pulled off the highway, parked, and then headed down the trail to the pond where the ice was smooth and hard, and the lake bottom was in clear view. At the forest-pond edge, only Brown hesitated, uncertain at first about walking on ice that looked like water. We all skated, and later on played shinny hockey with the kids, before gathering by a fire to drink hot chocolate.

Sarah smiled broadly when her two-and-a-half-year-old Abel exclaimed with excitement "Brown, all of your people are here!"

"Brown brings people together. Folks who love Brown love each other. We are Brown's people," Stephanie explained.

Back in 2016, for a whole bunch of reasons, Stephanie knew she needed to reach out to make new friends, but wasn't up to putting herself 'out there'. Newfoundland, where Steph trained to be a nurse, and then married and planned to raise children, was a very long way from Whitehorse. But she and hubby Duncan jumped in with both feet when

Newfoundlander friends, who'd moved to Whitehorse a few years back, decided to sell their rural property. Feeling ready for adventure, they found jobs in Whitehorse, Duncan as a paramedic and Stephanie as a nurse, and relocated from way east to way west.

While on maternity leave with her second son, Stephanie was feeling estranged from both local co-workers and her faraway east coast friends and family. Looking back, she had moved, for one reason or another, frequently and often far. Feeling disconnected was not all that surprising. Stephanie was homesick and not ready to meet new people or invest in new friendships.

"Really, I just wanted to move back home. Longing for Newfoundland, I was stuck in Whitehorse with the baby blues. I was feeling a bit sorry for myself and unmotivated to reach out and find new friends," Stephanie recalled.

One day at the Canada Games Centre in Whitehorse, while her first son (a curly red head like mom) played in the rec centre's toddler room, Stephanie perched by the window and watched idly as folks came and went. Her curly red locks tied snugly at the nape of her neck and dressed comfy in loose-fitting jeans and a big T-shirt, Stephanie felt cocooned in her loneliness. Then, suddenly, something outside interrupted her reverie. Up the hill in front of the Games Centre, on a bicycle, came a peddling mom, wearing Carhartt's, pulling one kid behind in a chariot trailer, and pregnant with #2.

"That's someone I'd like to be friends with," Stephanie muttered to herself.

She'd seen, Rose, with her long dark hair tied back, once

before, running laps around the indoor track while her young son snoozed in a corner.

"That's a mom maneuver I would do, no hesitation," Stephanie spoke to herself.

But Stephanie wasn't ready to introduce herself. Weeks passed as she worked up the nerve to break through the barrier that held her back from reaching out to make new friends. In the meantime, Rose's Sawyer and Stephanie's Connor were in the same rec centre preschool program. Stephanie watched Rose and Nicole, and noticed how much their boy, Sawyer, loved jam, and how much Rose and partner Nicole loved hugging their jam-faced boy.

Finally, Stephanie accumulated sufficient nerve and boldness to approach Rose, and mumbled something like, "Can me and my boy be friends with you and your boy?" Thus began a friendship between kindred souls.

Through years of friendship, the two families have met up many times: in the summertime to fill buckets with wild blueberries and chatter nonstop; in the fall for group playtime at Whitehorse playgrounds; and, during the long, cold Whitehorse winters, for sledding, cross-country skiing, and skating on lake ice.

Though the details of playdates have faded with time, Stephanie can easily recall the first sparks of what would become "a slow rekindling, at last, of the warmth of the Newfoundland community that I'd left behind."

As women and mothers, Rose and Stephanie, and Sarah, too, value hard work, eating well, reducing waste and needless consumption, saving money, and free play time outdoors with kids. In sharing these values, these three women inspire each other to be active, strong, capable, energetic, and independent.

About two years into their friendship, Rose asked Stephanie if she might keep Brown for a week and a bit while his winter keepers, Sarah and Jeffrey, were out-of-town. Rose let Stephanie know about Brown's wild streak, that he could be aggressive around both small dogs and small game. Stephanie said "yes" but with little dog experience, she also felt apprehensive about bringing Brown indoors with her boys. Brown arrived on the night of the Winter Solstice, and by a warm fire, on a clear, cold night, Stephanie's family fell in love with Brown. In the days that followed, Brown was gentle with her boys, and filled a void that the family hadn't noticed. As soon as Brown returned to his winter home in Haines Junction, Stephanie started looking for a Labrador puppy.

The following spring, Stephanie agreed, again, to take Brown for a few days. This time, Sarah and Jeffrey wanted to drop off Brown on their way to the Whitehorse airport, and the timing coincided with afternoon pickup time at Stephanie's boys' school. On the day of the handover, in the school parking lot, Brown's winter family was visibly worn down after traveling from Haines Junction with a son who was unhappy about being in the car. Brown, thankfully, was excited to see Stephanie and her boys. That schoolyard meeting with Sarah and Jeffrey also triggered a memory. As a community post-partum nurse, Stephanie had traveled out to Haines Junction to welcome Sarah and Jeffrey's first-born son!

After a few more Brown pick-ups and drop-offs, in Whitehorse and in Haines Junction, a friendship was springing up among Sarah, Stephanie, Rose, and their families.

One hot summer day, Rose and her boys, Stephanie and hers, and Brown, too, drove to the outskirts of town to cool off in Fox Lake. By chance they ran into Min and Steph and kids Molly, Gus, and Noah who were on leave from Australia to spend time with Canadian friends and family. It was a rare hot, windless Whitehorse day that drew them all of them out to Fox Lake.

"Brown seemed much older," said Min, "but he was still a very affectionate dog and had his crazy youthful energy. He came right up to me, and honestly, I felt a sense of knowing, that Brown indeed remembered me."

Steph was especially delighted that the one of their three offspring who'd been fearful of dogs, was comfortable around Brown. While the party was busy devouring cold melon and dunking in the lake to cool off, Brown dug a shallow depression and laid down in his soil nest for a cool snooze.

"When I'm feeling blue," says Stephanie, "I think back to that day at Fox Lake and feel gratitude that I am one of Brown's people."

During the big-snow winter of 2020, Stephanie and her friend Jen met up with Rose, Sarah, and Brown for a 20-kilometre cross-country ski. It was a record year for powder snow, the skiing was great, and all four laughed hard when Brown stepped off the packed trail and sank, to his surprise, into more than a metre of snow! Typically, in Whitehorse there's a metre and a bit of snow on the ground, but that year snow depth was closer to two metres.

Of the times Stephanie and her family kept Brown, and

occasionally Sarah and Jeffrey's dog Niija, too, Stephanie said, "Brown was always, well, Brown!! A bit comical, well-behaved, and well-loved especially on hikes when he zoomed off but returned frequently to check on his people."

In large measure due to their positive experience with Brown, Stephanie's family got a Labrador puppy that they named Lupin. But Brown was still welcome! Despite the difference in age between young Lupin and older Brown, when the two were together, the game of chase was fast and furious.

A Trip to Muncho

At the end of Brown's last field season, in 2021, he was sleeping well, so back he went to his winter home in Haines Junction. In early 2022, Brown stopped eating, and was brought to Whitehorse to see a vet. After getting a clean bill of health, Brown stayed on in Whitehorse with Rose. Over the previous year, Rose moved out of the house shared with Nicole and into a house shared with Taylor. Taylor, with two half-time kids of his own, was happy to take in a dog, and Rose was happy to have Brown around during the transition from full-time to half-time parent. For his part, Brown was happy to go on walks, sleep through the night, and when his food was softened with broth, to eat well, too. When home was busy and loud with four kids knocking around, Brown retreated to a corner. Through the rest of that year, Brown went back and forth, every few weeks or so, between Rose's place in Whitehorse and Sarah's home in Haines Junction.

As Brown neared the end of his life, Rose said, "He remained loyal and obedient to his people, and seemed to enjoy his new, easier town life."

The field season of 2022 was Rose's first without Brown. Her stint in the mountains was shorter than usual, three weeks instead of the usual six to eight. As was her habit in summers past, during the day, Rose didn't think of Brown unless she encountered a herd of twenty or so caribou, or a group of five or six rams or ewes. In the past, the appearance of wild animals would have made her pause to watch Brown's reaction.

Rose also thought of Brown, of course, when it was time to get into the truck or helicopter and head back to camp, to feed him, or to call him to the tent for the night. In those moments, Rose thought "Oh yes. Brown is not here." For Rose, the profound changes occurred the summer before, in 2021, during their last field season together when she wrote him the letter that described how he had contributed so meaningfully to her life.

Near the end of the 2022 field season, I flew north to be with Rose's two boys for the last week of her field work. At the end of that week, we packed up and headed to our Muncho Lake digs for a family camp-out. Sawyer, Sully, Rose and I, and her new partner Taylor and his children Clara and Ben who, respectively, were one-year and three-years older than Sawyer, came from Whitehorse. Brown was at Sarah's and stayed behind in Haines Junction with Jeffrey and the kids while Sarah worked at the park. I took the car that I leave up north, filled with my own gear and some of theirs, too. Virginia, who also lives in Whitehorse, was away on a different adventure, cycling from Tuktoyaktuk to Dawson City and back. My daughter Carolina and husband Blake, their boys Jaxson and Mason, and my daughter Melinda and her two-month-old Audrey came from Fort Nelson. Melinda's husband Bryan planned to join the Muncho camp at the end of his workweek. At Muncho, Rose's crew slept in a canvas wall tent, Carolina's family in their fifth wheel trailer, and Melinda, baby, and her two Yorkies in her small, towed camper. I slept alone in a two-person nylon tent. No one slept in the new log cabin, or in the old skid shack that Rose and Brown shared back at the beginning of their decade-long companionship.

The weekend was filled with six kids playing hard: fishing, hot springing, hoola-hooping with hoops the boys and I made in Whitehorse, racing trucks and trikes down the big hill, and playing chess on the cabin's deck. We hiked across the rock and boulder strewn alluvial fan to drink from the creek and haul water back to camp, scrambled up and down steep mountain slopes, smoked fish and moose meat, and tossed bean bags. Mason and I cycled along the highway and through the provincial campground and stopped to skip stones across the lake. Rose and crew took the canoe down to the water's edge but found the wind too strong and the lake surface too rough for paddling. With each of my daughters, I walked and talked. Melinda's two-month-old baby Audrey got a lot of snuggles.

Thirty-two years ago, in 1990, it was mid-summer when two-month-old baby Melinda first visited Muncho Lake. Six months later, I left the north with my four daughters in tow. Unlike her sisters, who were older by seven, nine, and eleven years and were youngsters during my time in the north and then returned each summer, Melinda spent her growing up years with me in southwestern BC, central Alberta, and southern Ontario. But like her sisters, Melinda moved back to the north. "I wanted to be close to family and part of a small-town community where life is slower paced and more affordable than in the big city. I wanted to settle down in the place I was from. I love my life in Fort Nelson." In the mountains, weather can quickly change, it's hot during the day and cold at night, sunny in the morning and stormy in the afternoon. Nevertheless, new momma and baby camped with us for two nights. Our family camp out at Muncho Lake would strengthen, I hoped, family ties and breathe fresh love into mother-daughter and sister-sister bonds.

For me, it was also a time of transition. During that visit to Muncho, in summer 2022, I felt, for the first time, ready to knock down the old skid-shack that was our first Muncho cabin. The roof was partially caved, and rats and squirrels had laid waste to floors and furniture. With my son-in-law Blake, tentative plans were made to pull out the wood cook-stove and heater, the wrought-iron sinks, and the single-pane windows, and then knock down walls and haul the cabin debris south to the Fort Nelson dump. With little or nothing of the old skid-shack worth saving, it was time for me to let go of 'my' Muncho and pass it on to my daughters, their spouses, and my grandchildren to renew and make their own. It was around then that I altered the Muncho deed to include my daughters.

Once I dreamt of using the old cabin as a writer's shack but never did. Two years ago, on a winter drive from Whitehorse to Fort Nelson, I spent two nights in the new log building. After cleaning and warming it up, I sat by the fire and wrote, through tears, about my life and times at Muncho Lake. In the summer of 2022, after everyone left the family camp for home, I sat, alone again, in the new cabin, this time by the window overlooking the lake. As the late afternoon sun streamed in, I wrote an ending to the story of *A Wild Life and A Dog Called Brown*. Like the old skid shack, Brown was old, and his looming end was on our minds.

For Rose, the family camp of 2022 was a rare visit back to the log cabin she started building more than ten years ago, with a surprise puppy by her side. Rose found it hard, emotionally, to confront the partial failure of her effort to build a sturdy log cabin that despite infrequent use would be free of pesky packrats. The cabin is sturdy indeed, good-looking, and functional with a sleeping loft, expansive front deck, and well-stocked kitchen. But to the packrats in the neighbourhood it became an extension of their home range. Feeling somewhat optimistic, Rose made tentative plans to return in the fall, lift the roof, and make the cabin rat-proof.

To ease Rose's considerable disappointment, I swept and bleached the log cabin's floors and surfaces, and before leaving, hung foamies, and scooped up bedding and linens for a town-washing at Melinda's in Fort Nelson, where I headed next. On my trip back to Whitehorse, I packed the clean bedding, and clean dishes into bins donated by Melinda and Bryan.

The inner force that drove Rose to build, alone, a log cabin at Muncho—fierce independence, youthful desire to achieve with her own physical strength and will-power, and determination to ensure her own happiness by taking care of her own needs and wants—has softened. At forty, Rose opened up about how the changes. "I still operate mostly like that, that is, fiercely independent (as Rory called me), except now I have deeper appreciation for the support a life-partner offers. This realization came as I felt pummeled by my own aging, a marriage breakdown, dad's passing, and the waning of Brown's life. Now, I feel more strongly that having a partner enriches life, has enriched mine, and brings a fullness to living that I wouldn't trade for anything else, that I wouldn't trade away to be independent, not even fiercely independent. Having someone to help me get through the day, the week, or the year is something I no longer push away, but welcome. Leaning on the people around me to get through hard times is humbling and, in turn, I have softened, become more empathic, less judgemental, and overall, more appreciative of friends, family, and partners (both past and current). Quenching the fierceness of my independence was not, after all, the sacrifice I imagined it might be, but instead allowed me to get closer to things that lie at the heart of being human, at the core of what it means to live happily and well."

The log cabin stands on a knoll above Muncho Lake, beside an aging skid-shack that is surrounded on three sides by a forest of stunted spruce trees, and moss mounds that each fall are dotted with bright red low-bush cranberries best picked after the first frost. 'My' Muncho—the cold, harsh, wild place where I got my first toehold in the world—is re-nested now into the hands and hearts of my children and grandchildren. That it will live on as a place where family gathers and together loves life is my wish.

The nostalgia that rode shotgun with me on this writing journey with Rose and Brown, to the past and then back to the present, and on trips to Muncho and back to Fort Nelson and Whitehorse, added to my enjoyment of it all. Neither melancholy nor loneliness lingered, as new pleasures slipped in to take their place. One of the new pleasures are the Brown stories and anecdotes shared by Rose and Brown's people, and especially the two women from Newfoundland and Nova Scotia, Stephanie and Sarah, who cherish, as Rose does, physical strength, motherhood, and independence. For the opportunity to share those stories here and reflect on the meaning of Brown's life to all of us, and to share my part of the story, I am grateful.

Brown's Last Day

Crying, trying hard to accept that an old and faithful friend was gone from the world, Rose wrote:

Life was too full, too hard, and I was too tired, frazzled, and emotionally distraught to get organized for Brown's last day.

On Brown's last day, I chose to not go to work. I drove the Ol' Grey Dog because Brown loved sitting beside me in that truck. Faithful work and adventure companion, Brown never wanted to be left behind and was excited when I lifted and set him down on the front bench seat. It had been a while since Brown was able to get into the truck on his own and, as usual, he seemed happy to have help. We toured the town, I grabbed a coffee from my favourite cafe, and then pulled into the Yukon Geological Survey parking lot where Nicole and the boys were waiting. They said goodbye to Brown, and then he waited in the Ol' Grey Dog while I drove Nicole's truck to the airport and back. Their trip to Vancouver to celebrate Nicole's birthday would distract the boys, I hoped, so they wouldn't get too worked up over their last physical connection with Brown.

Back at my work parking lot, I realized I'd brought nothing to wrap Brown in and wouldn't feel alright with his expired body exposed to the weather in the truck box. Then I remembered Brown's old field bed was stored in the gear room and after digging around also found an old tent cover that I never use. I tossed the bed and cover into the back of the truck.

The next stop was the vet's office and, looking back, that was the most difficult part of our last day together. Talk about people who are not my people! As we sat in the waiting room, a half dozen folks spoke one after another with each other and with staff with unabashed devotion to their amazing, cute, skinny, large, and small pets. In the moment, the oohs and ahs struck me as absurd. Brown had been loved and appreciated but with a sense of practicality, and with acknowledgement that Brown was a dog, not a human. Amidst the lively banter and bragging about wonderfully alive pets, it became impossible to hold back tears. No one seemed to notice my misery, and no one offered support to the dog and pet owner who would not be going home together.

It didn't get easier when it was our turn. The vet was kind, but too kind, and overly accommodating. In that moment, I wanted this part to go quickly, to not spend time giving Brown more hugs and more petting. When the moment arrived, Brown resisted the anesthetic and required a bear-hug while the vet administered the needle. Instantly, he fell asleep, and just as quickly he died. With the blanket the vet provided, we carried Brown out to the truck. I wrapped him in his old field bed and covered his limp body with the tent cover. Then off we went to our place in the country, a forty-five-minute drive from town.

The rest of the day was especially memorable but no less challenging. First, Virginia and I spent an hour dragging over logs to make a fire big enough to thaw the frozen ground. Thawing took a couple of hours. It lightened our mood when neighbour Steve dropped by to see how we were managing. We couldn't ignore the humor of the no-show backhoe, such a typical Cobbett comedy thinking you've got things organized to make life easy and, in the end, find a way to get the job done some other harder way. Dad would have said, 'When the going gets tough, the tough get going.' By the light of the dwindling fire, Virginia and I dug by hand, for a couple of hours, taking turns until the grave was big enough to hold Brown.

From the truck, which was parked nearby, we moved Brown onto a board. Lowering Brown's furry black body into the four-foot pit, I was overwhelmed with sorrow, but when his body was nested in the warmed earth, covered, and the hole refilled, I felt a weight lift from my shoulders.

The last year or two of my life has so often felt so hard, emotionally, that I found relief in getting this outstanding chore, Brown's end-of-life, done.

As the fire and the day of Brown's passing wound down, in memory of dad, Virginia and I drank a whiskey and coke. We talked about life as the last coals and the last of Brown died away, together. We laid down a few rocks to mark Brown's grave and headed indoors.

The day of Brown's passing—I won't ever forget. The bonds that Brown created among family and friends—will live on. For the dog, Dad, I will always be grateful.

Final Thoughts

I have spent a lot of time thinking about the places and events that underlie the memories that comprise my inner life, all the stuff that make me 'me.' I find remarkable that memories flung across the space and time between birth and now fit neatly inside my head where life's breadth and depth can be surveyed at any moment. There's a fluidity to memory, its timeline disassociated from aging, and its map disconnected from the places one has been. The measure of a life, it seems to me, is neither number of years lived nor tally of places one has been but the story that unfurls from memories detached from time and place. Life is like a sailboat underway, winds sometimes push, at other times pull, seas sometimes part in silence, other times in fury.

What has writing down the story of Brown's life meant to me? With one's passing, memories also pass. So, perhaps the written story of Brown and his people, of the intangible kinship that formed among far-flung individuals, children and adults, through love for a dog who seemed able to love back in equal or greater measure, will outlast both Brown the dog and Brown the memory. If in a story there lies proof that a life—dog, or human—has been a decent one, then may this story be proof that Brown was a remarkable, companionable, at times indispensable dog who founded a human family that lives on after his passing.

Brown, it seems, was extraordinarily good at doing what was asked of him by his several human keepers. Brown noticed and responded to a range of cues from a range of companions. He navigated successfully among a small party of humans, sometimes over long distances in remote places. *A Wild Life And A Dog Called Brown* shows how Brown and his people found the reciprocity of their relationship both rewarding and joyful.

In these ways Brown seemed to fit what researchers have found to be generally true about dogs. Brian Hare and Vanessa Woods, co-writers of <u>The Genius of Dogs</u>, reported that a dog's genius is an ability to read human gestures and cooperate with their keepers. They liken the human-dog bond to the human-infant bond, which forms quickly even after short interactions with strangers. Brown's ability to bond with new people and respond appropriately to new situations seems consistent, too, with observations that dogs can learn and apply experience to new situations. That Brown, part Labrador Retriever, was extraordinarily good at navigation lines up with evidence about other (but not all) Retrievers.

In <u>E.B. White on Dogs</u>, which was based on White's personal dealings with dozens of canine companions, E.B. shared a belief that a companionable and indispensable dog was an accident of nature. By chance, Brown was adopted by a group of people, his people, whose needs were remarkably well matched to his natural canine talents, and whose human sensibilities happened to be a good match for each other. Family and kinship, it seems, can form for all sorts of reasons, some that have nothing to do with biological relatedness. Maybe, like remarkable dogs, strong kinship, and the joys of it, are an accident of nature.

For me, telling the story of Brown has led me to a new 'place,' a place where hard things slip by and joy slips in a little more easily, like the joy of losing ourself in the company of trees and of finding ourself in the company of kinfolk.

On day Rose asked me, "Mom, do you have a favourite place?" Without hesitating, I answered, "Yes. The north is my true home."

In life, as in writing this book, I have taken many liberties. A few close encounters with truth I hope I have had.

~Maggie Squires

About Rose Cobbett's Geological Research

Rose's Ph.D. research involves sleuthing out the details of how the super-continent Rodinia broke apart, some 500 million years ago. Rodinia, in part, separated along a rift that forced the North American craton away from the continents that were once attached to its western edge. In areas of Yukon and the Northwest Territories, the events that led to Rodinia's breakup are preserved in the nature of the bedrock.

The particular focus of Rose's research is magmatism that occurred at the margins of the continents that eventually broke away from Rodinia. To uncover when and how ancient magmatism occurred, Rose investigated volcanic rocks at eight different locations in eastern Yukon and western Northwest Territories

Her success in finding at these sites the mineral zircon (which is somewhat rare where rift magmatism occurred) allowed precise determination of the timing of magma production during volcanic episodes known to be associated with continental rifting. Dating 450-million-year-old rocks to an accuracy of 100,000 to 200,000 years, which can be done with zircon, is as good as dating gets in the study of ancient geological processes. Without zircon, the approximate age of past eruptions is derived from the stratigraphy of underlying and overlying outcrops.

In addition, at each of the eight locations, Rose examined depositional features and the geochemistry of volcanic rock to determine the depth of mantle melting and whether magma was contaminated with continental crust or ocean floor sediments.

By addressing the bigger picture question of what happens below the earth's surface when continents split along a mid-ocean ridge, Rose's doctoral studies can assist in furthering our understanding of earth's geological evolution and in locating minerals and hydrocarbons utilized by humans.

Acknowledgements

To Rose, Virginia, Sarah, Min and Steph, and Stephanie: For writing down your Brown stories, and allowing their inclusion in this book, thank you.

To Esther: For the painting of Brown in the mountains and creating the book cover, thank you.

To Virginia, Elizabeth, Anna, and Dawn: Thanks to Virginia Cobbett for saying 'yes' to my every reading and editing request, no matter the topic; to Elizabeth Buchanan who fixed grammar and 'tense' in an early version; to Anna Haltrecht who never said 'no' to reviewing a new version of the manuscript and each time provided feedback that improved it; and, to Dawn Marie Paley, a former high school buddy of Rose's now living and working in Mexico as a freelance journalist and editor of Ojala.mx, who happily talked with me about her publishing experiences, and read and gave me thoughtful feedback on the manuscript.

To Donaleen Saul: For enthusiasm that kept me going, feedback that helped shape the writing into an appealing read, and friendship that keeps my writer's wings flapping, thank you.

To Don Murphy: For happily proofreading the story about Rose, me, and Brown, thank you.

To Brown, and to Ted posthumously: If not for you, there would be no story to tell.

To Brown's people: To the humans who loved Brown, it has been my good fortune to meet you and hear your stories. It was Brown's good fortune to have you as kin.

I am grateful for these two accounts of life up the Alaska Highway:

1. *The McDonalds: The Lives & Legends of a Kaska Dena Family* by Alison Tubman;
2. *Beyond Mile Zero: The Vanishing Alaska Highway Community* by Lily Gontard & Mark Kelly;

and, for these three books about dogs:

1. *The Genius of Dogs* by Brian Hare and Vanessa Woods;
2. *E.B. White on Dogs* Edited by Martha White; and,
3. *Solitude, Connection, the Writing Life And a Dog Called Fig* by Helen Humphries.

Throughout this book, quotations indicate the actual words of storytellers, occasionally edited for length and clarity. Any misrepresentation of original stories is inadvertent. The views, thoughts, and opinions expressed in the text are mine as the narrator of the stories, and do not necessarily correspond with those of the individuals mentioned herein.

A Wild Life And A Dog Called Brown

ABOUT THE AUTHOR

Maggie Squires has a Ph.D. in limnology. Over the last decade, she's studied lakes, large and small, from Wabush Lake in Labrador to St. Mary Lake on Salt Spring Island, to Snap Lake in the Northwest Territories.

In 2007, Maggie arrived on Salt Spring Island by sailboat from Pedder Bay on Vancouver Island and decided to put down anchor. She spends summers gardening and cycling on Salt Spring, and winters in the Yukon, cross-country skiing, writing, and visiting with her four daughters, four grandsons, and a granddaughter.

On Salt Spring and outside Whitehorse, Maggie's home is a simple dwelling with a wood stove, and big windows that look out upon forest. *A Wild Life And A Dog Called Brown* is her first book.

www.ingramcontent.com/pod-product-compliance
Lightning Source LLC
Chambersburg PA
CBHW021012090426
42738CB00007B/756